With Me In Paradise

With Me In Paradise

With Me In Paradise

What Happens to You After You Die

DAVID E. SEIP

Leqach Publishing, Inc. • Langhorne, Pennsylvania
Leqach.com

WITH ME IN PARADISE
What Happens to You After You Die

Leqach Publishing
P.O. Box 1031
Langhorne, PA 19047
www.leqach.com

PAPERBACK ISBN: 978-1-7364043-0-0
EBOOK ISBN: 978-1-7364043-1-7

Cataloging-in-Publication data:

Names: Seip, David E., author.

Title: With Me in Paradise: What Happens to You After You Die | David E. Seip

Description: Langhorne, PA: Leqach Publishing, Inc. 2021

Identifiers: ISBN 978-1-7364043-0-0 (paperback) | ISBN 978-1-7364043-1-7 (ebook)

Subjects: LCSH: Religious Belief | Death | Eschatology | Intermediate State | Future Life

Library of Congress Control Number: 2021906473
Classifications: BT 826.6 2021 (print) | BT 826.6 (ebook)

Cover Photograph by Scott Rodgerson
Cover design by TSG, Inc.

Manufactured in the U.S.A.   5/2021

To my children
Kimberly, Christopher, Andrew,
Bethany, Matthew

Contents

Preface

While there are many books written on the subject of
death and dying, far fewer have been written on what
happens to you after you die. The reason is likely because
there is little consensus and no one credible has returned
from the dead to give us a full accounting. Many of those
who dare to write on the subject of the afterlife often do
so with much speculation and conjecture. Even those who
attempt to follow a theological approach to the subject tend
to wander off-course in favor of personal opinion. Access
to misleading information is easily acquired on the Internet.
YouTube authors claim to know what happens the moment
you die. Some say that you go immediately to heaven; others say you are asleep in the grave until certain things take
place. Some profess to know that there is no eternal hell
and, therefore, everyone will eventually ascend to heaven.
The assumption of immediate ascent to heaven by the dead
is usually supported by a quote from Jesus found in Luke
23:43, where he says to the redeemed thief hanging next to
him on the cross, "Today you will be with me in Paradise."
Without capturing the statement's proper context, they pre-
sume Paradise to be heaven.

What happens after we die? It's human nature to wonder about it. Sadly today most pastors never preach on the subject and are mostly ill-equipped to thoroughly teach it. The failure stems from today's seminaries which teach very little about biblical theology, and when they do it comes with a muddled sense of connectivity from Old Testament to the New. The failure of ministers is also subject to their general lack of understanding of the languages found in the early manuscripts used in the compilation of the Bible; choosing instead to rely upon the loose wording of the English translations when using such words as heaven and hell.

The fact is, the Bible does provide a clear understanding of the afterlife and its sequence of occurrences which begin at the moment of death. We can have assurance of what will take place once we leave this life.

The purpose of this book is to provide proof of that assurance and instill comfort to loved ones left behind. But the Bible also sounds a dire warning for those who casually treat God's teachings on the afterlife. The Bible is quite clear that there is both a heaven and a hell, and it gives plenty of warning for those who refuse to live this life according to God's rules in order to attain to the best possible results in the afterlife. For those who live within God's precepts there is abundant evidence of the comfort and hope awaiting them.

There is a sequence of events that takes place in the "next" life. It is explained in Scripture. This book presents the path to understand it. Reading this book will remove the mystery and concern about death. If you are a believer (according to the teachings of the Bible), then this book will provide assurance that death yields no mystery. To the contrary, death provides escape from the boundaries of this life and immediate passage into the comfort and boundless peace of your awaiting eternity.

The important distinctions between the spirit, soul, and body in this present life are explained in detail. What happens to each of the three parts of our being in the future life is also described in an understandable and enlightening way. Every human being will pass from this life into a new plane of eternal existence, but not every human will experience the joy of being in the presence of God. The pathway to God is not open to arbitrary assumption or speculation, because Scripture itself makes that process known. We cannot work our way into heaven, as some believe. There are no alternative paths to the top of the mountain, as others believe. There is one path to heaven, one path to hell, and one path to what the Bible describes as the Kingdom of God. Entrance into that kingdom is conditional upon conduct in this life which is said to produce reward in that kingdom. This book describes the basis upon which some will obtain that reward.

Nothing is conjectured. No personal opinions are offered. The Bible itself forms the context of this book and its opinions. The book's goal is to bring to light what is promised and what uniquely happens to our spirit, soul, and body after death as we each await our destiny.

Introduction

The Catholic Church has its teaching on the afterlife; the Protestant church as well—with each denomination claiming to harness truth while still leaving much to the realm of mystery. The Buddhists, Hindus, Muslims and Jews all disagree with each other on what to expect in the next world, while exhibiting some curious overlap of thought. For instance, Buddhists believe that after death a person is reincarnated as another being, thus creating a new life. That new life is dependent upon past conduct. Karma also plays a big part in determining what happens after this life. They believe there is no permanence to this life—that includes the soul. The spirit, however, lives on with its future form dependent upon our choices in this life. And since every life is on an endless journey in pursuit of nirvana, this process continues until perfect enlightenment and tranquility is reached.

Hinduism, on the other hand, is far more illusive, partly because there are many sects within the religion. Hindus believe in a soul that is immortal and imperishable, but it belongs to an eternal cycle of life and death. Similar to Buddhists, they believe that you can only break this cycle when you achieve perfect enlightenment. What happens to you in the afterlife is based upon the choices made here and now; and fascinatingly, the state of your mind at the time of death. The cause of death and your funeral arrangements also become factors in your afterlife. Rather than a choice of heaven or hell, a Hindu could enter into a lower, middle, or higher world. The lower world is reserved for evildoers in painful endurance. The middle world is reserved for the majority of people, while the higher world is for the righteous where they experience pleasure. Curiously, Hindus believe that the soul does not stay at any level permanently. It stays only long enough to learn an undefined lesson. Afterward the soul comes back to earth as either human or animal depending upon your prior life. For example, a bad person is likely to come back poor, or as a lower animal form; and a good person is likely to come back as something beautiful.

Muslims also believe that the soul lives on after death, dictated by the good deeds performed in this life. According to Islam, good deeds will benefit the soul after death, while bad deeds will cause eternal suffering. It is a monotheistic religion based on the teachings and doctrines regarding a supreme being known as Allah. Followers of Islam believe that a person's soul returns to the kingdom of Allah when they die. Therefore, a person must strengthen their spirit by doing good deeds and praying regularly. Those who reject religion in favor of material possessions and earthly pleasures are doomed to suffer eternally after death.

In Islam, heaven is described as a place of "gardens and rivers" and hell as somewhere made of "fire." Islam teaches about Judgment Day, or the Last Hour, describing events that will take place on earth before Allah returns to raise people from the dead and deliver the final judgment on all human beings. Muslims believe that they will remain in their graves until that day. Islam also teaches that Allah is forgiving towards people who lived bad lives and will let them enter "paradise" after they have been punished and shown themselves to be truly sorry.

It is evident that many faiths have definitive teachings about the afterlife. But in answer to the question "What happens after I die?" the Torah, the most important religious text for Jews, is surprisingly silent. Nowhere does it discuss the afterlife in detail. Over the centuries a few possible descriptions of the afterlife have been incorporated into Jewish thought. However, there is no definitively Jewish explanation for what happens after we die. The Torah doesn't pay much attention to the afterlife. Instead, it focuses on this world and how to live a life that is pleasing to God.

C.H. Spurgeon, in a sermon preached on Sunday morning, May 24, 1857, spoke of a future existence beyond this life for the Christian, saying: "How different will be the state of the righteous up there, from the state of the believer here! Here the Christian has to suffer anxiety. He is anxious to serve his Master, to do his best in his day and generation. His constant cry is—'Help me to serve thee, O my God,' and he looks out day after day, with a strong desire for opportunities of doing good. Ah! If he be an active Christian, he will have much labor, much toil, in endeavoring to serve his Master; and there will be times when he will say, 'My soul is in haste to be gone; I am not wearied *of* the labor, I am wearied *in* it.'" Spurgeon's thoughts of the afterlife in contrast to the here and now, are ones often pondered; especially as life draws to a close. But finding peace in death, rather than anxiety, is not often realized. Perhaps the many voices professing knowledge of the subject add to our confusion. Do we even believe in a life after death? Many do not. Many are fatalistic toward earth. We're born, we die, and that's it. Others believe that life is eternal but with many passes through death leading to another reincarnated life in a form to be determined by some external force of nature.

For many centuries the world has concerned itself with the protocols and procedures of dying well. Perhaps the earliest dated writings on the subject is to be found in the *Ars moriendi* ("The Art of Dying"). The Latin text dates from about A.D. 1415. It was widely read and subsequently translated into most European languages, becoming the guide for death and dying literature for many years. There was a "short version" published in the 1460s which was printed from carved blocks of wood for both text and images. It is predominantly a shorter version of the original "longer version." The first ten woodcuts are divided into five pairs. Each set depicts the devil presenting five temptations along with a corresponding picture depicting the proper solution to the temptation. The final woodcut shows a dying man successfully weaving his way through the temptations and being accepted in heaven, while the devil returns to hell. The *Ars moriendi* served mostly to comfort the dying and provide guidance to family and friends gathered around the deathbed. And while much has been written about death and dying over the centuries—with three-quarters of a million books still in print related to the subject—the general subject of the "afterlife" consists of far fewer. It does not seem that the imbalance is due to a lack of interest in what lies on the other side of life. Most likely the vastly smaller number of books on the afterlife is due to the invisible nature of the subject. No one has come back from the dead to describe their experience—except a handful of those who report near-death experiences with differing phenomena and degrees of believability.

It is alleged that when Madam Roland was about to be executed in 1793, she stood before the guillotine and asked for writing material and the delay of her execution for a few minutes that she "might record the strange thoughts that were rising in her mind." How we might have welcomed the thoughts of her mind so near the prospect of her death. We cannot help but imagine that as a person approaches the separation of his present form and anticipates his future being, that some light must escape through the gloomy portal and rest upon the anxious traveler as he begins the journey to what lies beyond. Such would be a true revelation to a world hungry for some knowledge of death. Sadly, we only possess, and can only hope for, approximation in this life. Whatever a dying person might be envisioning, he is at that moment incapable of verbalizing its actual force.

According to the World Health Organization, about 56 million people die each year, which is an average of 153,424 people per day. The majority die from heart related causes and stroke. The United States ranks forty-third in life expectancy in a list of one hundred and ninety five countries. Spain currently ranks number one. The average lifespan in the United States is nearly eighty years of age. Yet, there is no guarantee of reaching even that milestone. And even if all humans were capable of it, what measure is this achievement against the realm of eternity?

Thoughts of eternity naturally mingle with thoughts of

the afterlife; and our understanding of what lies beyond—if anything—affects how we live. The possibility of reward or punishment beyond this life has served for millennia to shape the character of the living. Going back in history thousands of years reveals that there was hope of an afterlife and the separate existence of the soul even during the time of the Egyptian pharaohs. If any connection is to be traced between the funeral care of the Egyptians and their belief in the separate existence of the soul, there cannot be any doubt that there also existed a doctrine of immortality. That such a connection existed is confirmed by a remark of Diodorus Siculus, the first century Greek historian, concerning the inhabitants of Egypt. "These people," he assures us, "regarded the term of human life as bounded by very narrow limits, and therefore manifested the greatest anxiety to leave behind them a high reputation for virtue." With this thinking, they called their lives dwellings of the living *tents*, because they were to occupy them for only a very short time; whereas they termed the tombs of the dead eternal mansions, since they were to pass an infinite period of time with the gods below. For the same reason they were less careful about the structure of their houses; while their tombs were lavished with much more care. It was also evident that the lives of most were not sufficiently pure to justify the expectation of an immediate enjoyment of celestial happiness. It appeared necessary that the contaminated soul should undergo a process, which recognized a hatred of sin that somehow must be washed away. Thus the purified soul would eventually return to its original body where it would be permitted to enjoy its ultimate bliss, as part of the "great soul" of the world.

It is obvious that religious and secular worldviews have distinct yet occasional overlapping thoughts of the afterlife. Who's right? What source do you turn to for assurance of facts? The wisest approach for any serious research is to search the oldest and most reliable reference source. Irrefutably, the Bible is that document. It is the oldest document of recorded history. It describes God as the infallible source of all things visible and invisible. Some may resist the existence of God, but their conclusion cannot be defended against the supernatural exposition of his written Word. There is a presumption in its favor. If there is a God anywhere in the universe, and if we are his creation, he would surely not leave us in doubt concerning the great problems which have to do with our spiritual and eternal life. Plato lamented that he was adrift on a raft upon an open sea with no rudder, no star above to guide him; yet he, pagan though he was, maintained the hope that eventually, "the gods would give us a staunch boat to sail in." This was the expression of a universal thought. If there is a God he would surely reveal himself to his children.

How can we trust the Bible's claims regarding a future life when no one living has ever seen or experienced it? How can the statements be verified? They can only be verified if we believe the source of information to be trustworthy. For something supernatural, the source must have firsthand knowledge of the supernatural. That puts the focus of the source upon God. To question the existence of God, or the Bible, or his means of communication is futile. There has yet to be a satisfactory explanation to God's nonexistence. The Bible has never been satisfactorily refuted. How can it be refuted. It is an inexplicable collection of writings that are supernaturally inspired, and the Bible claims to be just that, leaving no doubt as to its inspiration. The word in the Greek is *theopneustia*, "breathed of God." The Bible says, in explicit terms, "All Scripture is breathed out by God and profitable for teaching, for reproof, for correction, and for training in righteousness, that the man of God may be competent, equipped for every good work." (2 Timothy 3:16–17). And it speaks no less definitively as to the method of its inspiration. "For no prophecy ever came by the will of man; but men spoke from God, being moved by the Holy Spirit."

If the Bible is not true, then it sets up a fraudulent claim; but if that claim can be verified we have no alternative but to receive it at its face value and frame our lives accordingly. The question, pro or con, must be determined by internal evidence. Therefore, if you open the Bible you will find that the proof of its inspiration is as satisfactory as that which it declares to substantiate—such as the immortality of the soul, and the divinity of Christ. The Bible is a volume made up of sixty-six books, on a large variety of themes, written by forty-plus writers of various tongues and nationalities, writing at intervals along a period of sixteen hundred years without any possibility of collusion. Yet the sixty-six books when bound together constitute a harmonious and consistent whole; yielding one non-contradicting system of doctrine. The conclusion is irrefutable.

The Bible is the only book that touches and solves every one of the great problems that have to do with human destiny. You cannot ask a question concerning God, or immortality, or salvation which it does not answer—and answer so clearly as to satisfy the simplest mind. There was never to be an addendum, no errata, no second edition to the Bible. Augustine was one of the greatest theologians to ever live. He wrote volumes on theological truths, but in later life was forced to make corrections to his earlier thoughts. Here is the oldest book in the world. A portion of it was old when Egypt was founded. The Book of Job had been written three thousand years when Chaucer, the father of English literature, wrote The Canterbury Tales. The Book of Ruth was twenty-five hundred years old when America was discovered. Yet there are hundreds of millions of people who read their Bibles routinely and find it fresh and satisfying for daily needs. That is because the Bible was fashioned in the beginning to all the change and circumstance of time and progress of the coming ages. Its truths, its ethical precepts, its great and precious promises have stood the test of time. It might be supposed that a book dealing with spiritual truths, all of which lie beyond the purview of the physical senses, would speak with some measure of reserve or uncertainty; but there are no "ifs" or "perhaps." We want no guesses about life and immortality. We want authority, and there can be no final authority with respect to these problems except a divine proof.

If the critics were to be taken at their word we would be asked to agree that the Bible is full of frightful errors. Its prophecies have failed, its history is not historical, its science is unfounded, its stories are myths, its facts are outlandish. In short, say the scoffers, there is practically nothing trustworthy in it. To the contrary, the critics have not been able to produce a single error or discrepancy which cannot be easily and accurately explained. Of its ten-thousand prophecies not one has yet failed. The history in the

Bible is the only infallible history of the world, and that history remains in tact even though it has stood the test of long centuries of criticism. Archaeologists are unearthing confirmation of its history every day. It used to be said, for example, that the Battle of the Four Kings was purely a fable, and then a person dug up a royal library in the valley of the Euphrates, bearing the date of 640 B.C. In that library were found the names of the Four Kings. And it is worthy of note that two hundred years ago there were more than eighty so-called "scientific theories" placed before the French Institute, every one of which was alleged to contradict Scripture. Where are they now? All have died their death.

One of the earliest books of the Bible to have been written is the Book of Job. In it there is a dialogue recorded between God and Job. God asks Job a question concerning death: "Have the gates of death been revealed to you?" Essentially God is asking Job what he knows about the life beyond, since he neither created life nor experienced what lies beyond the visible world. Because this is one of the earliest books, Job would not have had much Scripture to fall back upon in searching out an answer to God's workings. We, however, have much more knowledge of God than Job, and we are told quite a lot about what lies beyond the grave. Notwithstanding, much confusion arises from interpretations of what God is actually saying about death. As a sample, here are a few interpretations of theologians from the nineteenth century—a time period of heightened interest in the future life. One theologian remarked, "We believe that life, in connection with the gospel in the Word of God, means life, or a perpetuation of the existence of the creature man; and that death means death, or an extinction of the existence of the creature man." I have spoken with many people who think that once you die that's the end of existence; there's nothing else. Years ago there was a television commercial that reminded its potential consumers that "you only go around once."

Another notable theologian remarked, "We have only to open our dictionaries, no matter in what language, in order to find that, invariably, the primary meaning attached to death is non-existence." Still another said, "We thus see, that Scripture speaks of death in exactly the same way that it is spoken of in common life—not as a 'condition of existence' or life, but as the direct opposite of existence or life." In other words, you stop *being*. What is affirmed by these theologians is that death introduced non-existence. Merriam-Webster dictionary defines the primary meaning of death as, "That state of a being, animal, or vegetable, but more particularly of an animal, in which there is total and permanent cessation of all the vital functions; when the organs have not only ceased to act, but have lost the susceptibility of renewed action." Despite these claims, God's Word proves that *being* does not cease at the moment of death. To the contrary, something wonderful begins to happen.

CHAPTER 1

The Bible and Your Death

When we speak of death in a biblical sense, we must regard it from two points of view: death as a transition of passage; and, death as a state of existence. In other words, we must view death first as an event that takes place; a moment in time that ends life in its present context. This moment in time, once reached, is the vehicle God uses to usher in a new state of existence. This process of ending one state of life and transferring into a new one is the same process for everyone. No one will escape this process. No matter how you lived your life, the process is the same. It is not contingent upon how good you were in life, how hard you prayed, how often you went to church, how frequently you read your Bible, whether you were a practicing Muslim, the process is the same. However, the timing, events and outcome while entering into this new state of existence will vary based upon certain conditions met or ignored in this life. Once the process of death takes place, entering into a new state of existence is immediate and the sequencing of events irreversible. You can do nothing after death takes place to change the course through which your new state of existence will transport you.

Death, in the Bible, is properly and primarily spoken of as the moment the soul is out of the body. This takes place instantly. It is spoken of in the New Testament in John 4:47, "He was at the point of death." In Mark 5:23, we read, "My little daughter is at the point of death." This is the view given in the Merriam-Webster dictionary. Death as the point of passage, is called in the New Testament "an end." In Matthew chapter 2 it says, "He remained there until the death (end) of Herod," and also, "But when Herod died (was ended)." On the surface, one might argue that this proves that death is equal to non-existence. But it's not. Scripture speaks as we do of a person's *coming to his end*. But neither the Scriptures nor we mean anything but a "relative" end; an end to animal life, to the beating of the heart. And while the Bible speaks of King David's end in the Book of Acts 2:29 where it says, "I may say to you with confidence about the patriarch David, that he both died and was buried," the author goes on to teach, that David's soul is left in Sheol (Hades in the Greek). But, according to God, the soul is the man. The soul leaves the body at the moment of physical death. David therefore exists. His end is only an end relative to this earthly life and the body.

Death is not absolute. 2 Corinthians 5:1 says—"For we know that if the tent, which is our earthly home, is destroyed, we have a building from God, a house not made with hands, eternal in the heavens." Man is dissolved (detached) at death, when he is divided into body, on the one hand; and soul and spirit on the other—severed from the body, disconnected. Death as the point of passage is a departure. So we speak of the dead as "deceased," or "departed." Philippians 1:23, 24 says, "My desire is to depart and be with Christ, for that is far better." 2 Timothy 4:6 says, "The time of my departure has come." All of these views of death suppose that after the moment of death there comes the state of death. A person's death is relative, not absolute. A person's end is only his end in relation to this world; he is still existing somewhere else. There is an end here, but there is a beginning in another place. The tent is taken down here; but the occupant has moved elsewhere. The person has only departed. He still exists. He has gone to "Sheol" (in the Hebrew language), or "Hades" (in the Greek). We will explain this location in the next chapter.

Life has ceased, but "life" and "existence" are two different things. If life is a state of being, so is death. Death proper is the act of passing from the one to the other. The act precedes the state—it introduces it. Nowhere in the Bible does death mean non-existence. The Bible never says the body dies. It says the "person" died, but not the "body" died, because death affects the whole person. The Book of Numbers says, "The men which Moses sent to search the land...even those men...died by the plagues." Numbers 20:28 says, "And Aaron died there on the top of the mountain." 1 Samuel 25:1 says, "Now Samuel died. And all Israel assembled and mourned for him, and they buried him in his house at Ramah." The Bible speaks of the soul dying. "Let me (my soul) die the death of the upright," said Balaam in Numbers 23:10. "And Samson said, let me (my soul) die with the Philistines," in Judges 16:30. It is not true, then, that whenever the Bible speaks of death, it affirms the non-existence of that which is said to be dead.

Another issue concerning death is that it occurs only

once. Hebrews 9:27 states, "...it is appointed for man to die once, and after that comes judgment." The context of this statement is that death is the portal to judgment. And that judgment" is "eternal." God's primary purpose for death is to advance our spirit, soul, and body forward to the point of judgment. Death creates the passage to achieve judgment. The purpose of judgment is to settle the place of the person forever in his new and eternal state of existence. After judgment there is no death possible—in the sense of ending one's existence. Once the sentence of judgment is uttered, once begun to be received, we live with the consequence forever. But some might interject at this point that the Bible speaks of the "Second Death" which will be suffered by what it calls the "lost." They might say that these are to cease to exist, destroyed by the fire of wrath in the afterlife. The correct meaning of the Bible is that the Second Death is the prepared home of the lost, in which they are to find their heritage forever, even as the saved find theirs in heaven, the city of God. The Second Death is not a second physical death. Just as the redeemed have their home forevermore in what the Bible describes as the new Eden of God, so outside the city are to be forever the unclean and unredeemed. That is their Second Death. As the righteous dwell on the new earth, so in the Second Death dwell the lost. The Second Death cannot mean the second act of dying, because death is to be only once, even as Christ could die but once. Therefore, after death there is not non-existence, but judgment.

At the passage of death the body dies once but the soul and spirit live on. Jacob in Genesis 37:35 is reported to have said, "I shall go down to Sheol in mourning for my son."

What did Jacob mean by the reference to the pronoun I? What was the "I" referring to? It was Jacob's soul. "Whom shall I bring up to you?" asked the witch to Saul in 1 Samuel 28. "Bring up Samuel to me." "And Samuel said to Saul, why have you disturbed me by bringing me up?" What is the inference in the name Samuel? His body? No. It is his soul.

Spiritual death is quite different from actual, physical death. What is spiritual death? The person who is in spiritual death is still spiritually existent, though in an evil, unredeemed state. Spiritual death is not non-existence in spirit. The Bible speaks of the dead as existing. Luke 20:38 reads, "Now he is not God of the dead, but of the living, for all live to him." Jesus, in proving resurrection from God's calling himself "the God of Abraham," supposes that God meant by Abraham the man, as consisting of spirit, soul, and body. Now, we find that Abraham is divided. His body is in the cave of Machpelah. His soul and spirit are in Sheol. But one day the disjoined parts of Abraham will be brought together, and then he will experience what the Bible calls resurrection. The Bible says in 1 Peter chapters 3 and 4 that Jesus, as the departed spirit, preached to the departed spirits in prison, preached "even to those who are dead." And they heard and accepted his word. Christ himself is declared to be the firstborn of the dead, in Colossians 1:18. That supposes, then, that the dead are still in existence, though it is a secret (invisible) existence. Birth does not give life; it only manifests life that was eternally pre-existent. Conception does not create life; it only presents a pre-existent life in a new state of existence. Life is eternal. Life does not cease; only the state of life ceases.

The end of physical life here on earth does not introduce immediate transfer into heaven or hell, as many suppose. The deceased—all deceased—enter Sheol upon death. It is only a temporary location; but not in the sense that Purgatory is temporary, because Sheol is not a place to refine or purge the soul of sin. For the unsaved (or unregenerate) this temporary location is a place of torment. For the redeemed, it is a blissful location, one of greater bliss than this present life on earth. This is the location referred to by Christ when he used the expression "paradise," as when he assured the thief hanging next to him on the cross in Luke 23:43, "today you will be with me in Paradise." Paradise refers to a place laid out for pleasure. Jesus traces for us the soul's flight upon death to the places prepared when he tells his disciples the story of the rich man and the poor man in Luke 16:19–31. He said the poor man (named Lazarus) died, and was carried by the angels to Abraham's side. The rich man also died, and was buried, and in hell (Sheol) he lift up his eyes, being in torment. The rich man said, "Send Lazarus, that he may tell my five brothers, so they do not themselves come into this place of torment."

Yet there are those who would insist that this is merely a parable. It's allegorical in its intent. The people and details are symbols for something having deeper meaning. But, Jesus does not describe the story in that way. Is Luke attempting to convey its meaning in that fashion? The Bible conveys a different purpose. One simple proof is that no other story told by Jesus in the form of a parable gives the main character a name. Here we have a proper name given to the poor man; Lazarus. Some theologians prefer to say these are not real characters, that the rich man is representative of the Jew feasting sumptuously every day on God's spiritual riches, as set out in Moses and the prophets. They identify Lazarus as the Gentile full of sores representing the awful transgressions described in the Book of Romans, chapter one. The dogs that licked his sores are said to be Gentile philosophers.

In Jesus' narrative the rich man dies and we are told that he lifted up his eyes in torment after his death. In spite of that we are asked to assume that he represents the Jews still alive, and full of spiritual unrest. The rich man makes two requests: first for relief to himself through Lazarus. He pleads, "Send Lazarus to dip the end of his finger in water and cool my tongue, for I am in anguish in this flame." Is that consistent with what the Jews have been doing for two thousand years? Have they, as a people, been asking the ministers of the gospel to bring them relief? The rich man then asks his second request that warning may be given to his five brothers, who have not yet come to "the place of torment." If this is a parable filled with symbolic events shouldn't the number of brothers be ten, since that is the number of the lost tribes of Israel?

But Abraham is unyielding. He replies that Christ is not to go to them, that Moses and the prophets are enough to save them. It is more consistent with biblical theology to consider the idea that Jesus is speaking of facts over such metaphors. Jesus is not giving a revelation of the state of the dead. He is neither approving nor disapproving this story he is telling. He is merely providing a solemn warning to the Pharisees, because of their mocking attitude toward Him. The Pharisees might be as blameless outwardly as the rich man, and yet be lost inwardly because of unbelief in one greater (i.e., Jesus) than Moses. This theory that the story is only a parable with hidden meaning amounts to a thin veil of unbelief. The Bible reminds its readers that, "All Scripture is breathed out by God and profitable for teaching, for reproof, for correction, and for training in righteousness." (2 Timothy 3:16).

I make this point to show how contrary to the Bible are the muddled doctrines I am opposing concerning death, future life, and resurrection. We have reached a point in time were it has become necessary to confront more and more false scriptural testimony. Some might describe it as living in a time of unholy crusade. We must first know the truth concerning the afterlife.

Notwithstanding, there will be a moment of death for each of us. Historically we are intrigued by the notion of death. But it will not be an end, rather a new beginning; a moment of transit into a new state—a blissful state.

CHAPTER 2

Your Spirit, Soul, and Body

In the benediction included at the end of his first letter to the church in Thessalonica, the apostle Paul prayed that their whole spirit, soul, and body would be kept blameless at the coming of the Lord Jesus Christ. Why did Paul make a distinction between these three components of a person's being? The strongest reason for calling these three components of *being* to the church's attention is because of how intricately they are connected to eternal, future life. When the Lord returns to redeem his church a person's spirit, soul, and body will each participate in his return. There is no doubt that Paul's writings reflect his awaiting the certain return of the Lord. Whether it happened in his lifetime or not, he knew the Lord would return and he wanted the church to be blamelessly prepared in spirit, soul, and body when that happened. The distinction between the three components of being might have been clear to the church in Paul's day but it is not clear to us today. In this generation there is much confusion. People commonly believe that the spirit and soul are two words for the same thing.

At the moment of death your spirit/soul goes immediately to a place called heaven—or, at least, that's the concept planted in our minds by movies and novels. Without any thought, we are glad to simplify our understanding of the afterlife. You die, your spirit/soul goes to heaven from which we enjoy reunion with your loved ones.

In Genesis 1:26 the word translated for God is Elohim. The word is plural, and in the ancient Hebrew language it meant "three or more." The verse says, "let *us* make man." And it speaks of man being made in God's image. "Let us make man in our image, after our likeness." In the New Testament, in Matthew 28:19, the reader is presented with a threefold distinction of the Father, Son and Holy Spirit. In Matthew 3:13–17 the reader is also presented with the concept of Father, Son and Holy Spirit. There are ample other passages of Scripture which confirm the truth of the Trinity of the Godhead, God the Father, God the Son and God the Holy Spirit. Therefore, since Elohim is a "Trinity," for man to be created in the image and likeness of Elohim, he too must be a trinity. Since the Bible states that Jesus is Elohim manifest in the flesh, and since it says that the whole Godhead dwells in Him bodily, and it also says that Jesus was made in the likeness of his creature man (except for sin), then he too must be a trinity, like man.

It is in 1 Thessalonians 5:23 that the Spirit of God brings out the truth of man's threefold being, spirit, soul, and body. Hebrews 4:12 also distinguishes between spirit and soul. It reads, "For the word of God is living and active, sharper than any two-edged sword, piercing to the division of soul and of spirit, of joints and of marrow." Using our knowledge of Christ's incarnation, we would naturally expect spirit, soul, and body in the Lord Jesus Christ to likewise be distinguished. And, that is exactly what the Scripture teaches. When Jesus yielded up his spirit on Calvary's cross, his spirit went into heaven to God the Father (Luke 23:46). We also have the same experience at the time of the stoning of Stephen (Acts 7:59). Even in the Old Testament, in Ecclesiastes 12:7, we are told that the spirit returns unto God who gave it. It reads, "and the dust returns to the earth as it was, and the spirit returns to God who gave it." Furthermore, at the time of the Lord's death his soul went down into Paradise. You recall that he said to the thief hanging next to him—"today, you will be with me in paradise." He was referring to that restful part—or the place of the redeemed—in Sheol (the Hebrew word), or Hades (the Greek word), which was in the lower part of the earth. This is the same place where Lazarus and the rich man went. The rich man was detained in the part containing the lost, and the poor man Lazarus detained in the part containing the saved in Christ.

In Acts 2:27, the King James translation reads, "thou wilt not leave my soul in hell, neither wilt thou suffer thine Holy One to see corruption." In the Greek it is not the word "Hell." The word should correctly be translated "Hades," the temporary resting place. At the time of Christ's resurrection and later on at his ascension it appears that Paradise and its inhabitants were transferred from the lower regions of the earth into the third heaven. That explanation is found in Ephesians 4:8–10 where it reads, "When he ascended on high he led a host of captives, and he gave gifts to men. (In saying, "He ascended," what does it mean but that he had also descended into the lower parts of the earth? He who descended is the one who also ascended far above all the heavens, that he might fill all things.).” Consider 2 Corinthians 12:1–4, where Paul reveals that since the resurrection and ascension of Jesus, Paradise is in the third heaven. It reads, “I must go on boasting. Though there is nothing to be gained by it, I will go on to visions and revelations of the Lord. I know a man in Christ who fourteen years ago was caught up to the third heaven—whether in the body or out of the body I do not know, God knows. And I know that this man was caught up into paradise—whether in the body or out of the body I do not know, God knows—and he heard things that cannot be told, which man may not utter.”

At the time of his death, the body of the Lord was placed in the tomb of a man named Joseph and he remained there until the morning of his resurrection. Because his body was a sinless body it did not and could not see decay. All other bodies, like that of Job, returned to dust. Job, in Job 10:9 said, “Remember that you have made me like clay; and will you return me to the dust?” Also notice in the Gospel of John 11:39 that the body of Lazarus was in the process of returning to dust when Jesus raised him from the dead. Here is how this links together: From what I have just written, that at the time of the Lord’s death his spirit went to be with God the Father, his soul went into the Paradise-side of Sheol (or Hades), and his body went into the tomb in Joseph’s garden.

Consider the fact that in the so-called temptation of Christ—which is given to us in all four Gospels—the Lord says, “in all points like as we.” He means that he was tempted in spirit, soul, and body. In Matthew 4:1–4 he was tempted in his body to turn stones into bread to satisfy bodily hunger. In verses 5–7 his soul was tempted to make a great display before man of his supernatural power by hurling himself into space from the top of the temple. In verses 8–10 he was tempted in his spirit to worship Satan rather than God. Man also suffers from the threefold temptation to his spirit, soul, and body. In man's spirit there is found God-consciousness. In his soul there is found self-conscious. In his body there is found sense-consciousness. Man is not a simple, singular being but a compound being of three constituent parts—spirit, soul, and body. Paul's prayer for man was that he might in his "entirety" be sanctified in the Day of the Lord.

What is meant by the expression that someone is a soulish or natural person? It means that he is dominated by the workings of his soul. He is ruled by his own personal feelings, his own emotions, his own affections, his own passions, his own desires, his own likes and dislikes, his own will. A person like that is a soulish or natural man and he is unable to understand spiritual things because spiritual truths are spiritually discerned. The soulish man does not have spiritual discernment. As the Bible says in the Gospel of John, his spirit must be born from above to have such discernment.

What is meant by the expression that someone is a spiritual person? A spiritual person is one who is controlled by the Holy Spirit of God, acting through his own spirit according to the Word of God. The spiritual person controls his own feelings, his own emotions, his own desires, his own likes and dislikes, and his own will; whereas the soulish or natural person is controlled by his emotions, desires, passions, and appetites. 1 Corinthians 2:14 expresses this truth very clearly: "The natural person does not accept the things of the Spirit of God, for they are folly to him, and he is not able to understand them because they are spiritually discerned." Here the natural person is the soulish person, or the one who has not allowed control of his soul by his spirit dominated by the Holy Spirit.

1 Corinthians 2:14 and 3:1 reveal three classes of persons. First is the natural or soulish person—one who has not been born again (or, "born from above"). Second, is the carnal person—one who has been born again but is still an infant in Christ, being under soulish impulses and not in submission to the Holy Spirit of God. Third is the spiritual person—one who has been born again and whose body and soul are controlled by the Holy Spirit of God working through the person's spirit.

To be clear, the Holy Spirit of God does not present truth to our souls or bodies; that is, to our brain, reason, senses or intellect. He presents his truth directly to our spirits. Dr. Harold J. Ockenga (1905–1985), former president of Fuller Theological Seminary and a leading figure of mid-twentieth-century American Evangelicalism, said this in referring to 1 Corinthians 2:14, in his book, *Expository Values in Thessalonians*, "The soulish or natural man is contrasted to the spiritual man. The spirit of man holds communication with the unseen and is the seat of his God-consciousness. The soul is the seat of all affections, impulses, and is man's man-consciousness. The body links man to the material world and is the seat and instrument of his outward deeds and is the seat of his world-consciousness. Sanctification involves the whole man as is evidenced by the words holy, whole, blameless."

Dr. A.B. Simpson (1843–1919), the founder of the Christian and Missionary Alliance, in his book, *The Holy Spirit* said, "The predominate characteristic of the natural or soulish man is expressed by the word soul, just as the predominate characteristic of the new man in the New Testament is expressed by the word spirit. The soul represents the intellectual and emotional elements that constitute man. The spirit represents the higher and the divine life which links us directly to God and enables us to know and to come into relationship with divine things."

Dr. Richard C.H. Lenski (1864–1936), a German-born Lutheran pastor, in his commentary on the Epistle to the Hebrews said, "The soul (*psyche*) is the seat of the thoughts, emotions, feelings, desires, volitions and actions pertaining to our earthly and bodily existence. The spirit (*pneuma*) is the immaterial part of our being that was created and breathed into us by the breath of God, and is therefore the real seat of all his gracious operations in regenerating and renewing us. In the unregenerate, the soul (*psyche*) rules and the spirit (*pneuma*) is enslaved. In the regenerate this is reversed. The spirit (*pneuma*) is enthroned and the soul (*psyche*) is enslaved. Thus no longer are we ruled by our natural, earthly, sensual soul (*psyche*) but by our spiritual self (*pneuma*)."

Robert Govett in his commentary on the Book of Hebrews said, "Scripture distinguishes between the three parts of man—spirit, soul, and body. The soul is the seat of the instincts and passions which we possess in common with animals. The spirit is the deeper and more immaterial portion with which we serve God." As defined by these representative theologians the Bible distinguishes and separates the soul from the spirit.

If you own a good lexicon, a study of the three words, spirit, soul, and body can be very valuable. In the Hebrew the word for soul is *nephesh*, and in the King James translation of the Bible the word is unfortunately and indiscriminately translated as the words "life" and/or "soul." In the Greek the word for soul is *psyche*; and again, soul in the King James translation is also translated indiscriminately "life" and/or "soul." In Latin the word soul comes from the word *anima*, meaning that which animates the body, and is usually translated "life." For example, in Leviticus 17:11 we learn that the soul (or the life), nephesh, is in the blood. Hence the soul is that which gives life to our physical being. As Govett said, "this is true of animals as well."

A question naturally arises concerning the salvation of the soul. Peter, in the first chapter of his first Epistle makes the salvation of the soul (the natural life) dependent upon faithfulness after one's spirit has been saved. James 1:21 makes the salvation of the soul dependent upon laying aside the old person and putting on the new. Paul equates the salvation of the soul with winning rewards and dependent upon suffering and perseverance. Many Christians today, while being deeply appreciative of the eternal security they possess, wrongly imagine that it makes no difference how they live. They seem to think that all Christians will rule and reign with the Lord despite the fact that innumerable Scripture verses attest to the fact that positions of sovereignty in the coming kingdom of our Lord are determined by obedience, faithfulness, suffering and perseverance.

Regarding the spirit, it is saved at the time of the new birth (or regeneration). The body, however, is redeemed at the time of the rapture when Christians are transformed into new bodies. But the salvation of the soul, or the life of the person, is something dependent upon and determined by the individual himself as he seeks, follows and surrenders to the leading of the Holy Spirit.

So, to encourage Christians to live for the Lord after their salvation, the Lord has offered many rewards, including sovereignly ruling with him in the coming Kingdom (as described in a parable in the Gospel of Luke, chapter 19). The Book of Philippians 3:13–14 reads, "Brothers, I do not consider that I have made it my own. But one thing I do: forgetting what lies behind and straining forward to what lies ahead, I press on toward the goal for the prize of the upward call of God in Christ Jesus." 1 Thessalonians 5:23 says, "Now may the God of peace himself sanctify you completely, and may your whole spirit and soul and body be kept blameless at the coming of our Lord Jesus Christ." In the Book of Hebrews 4:12 we also read, "...piercing to the division of soul and of spirit." These verses along with others call to our attention man as a trinity.

God is a Trinity: God the Father, God the Son and God the Holy Spirit. Man was created in the image and likeness of God and of necessity man must be a trinity. "Then the LORD God formed the man of dust from the ground and breathed into his nostrils the breath of life, and the man became a *nephesh* (soul)." (Genesis 2:7). Man was formed from the dust of the ground; God breathed into him the breath of life, and man became a living soul. This verse from the Old Testament describes the three-part nature of man. In the New Testament we find a clearly articulated path to salvation. It declares that each of these three parts of man is subject to salvation, though at different times and in varying aspects.

The New Testament describes the salvation of the spirit. When Adam and Eve were first formed and created respectively, they had perfect communion with God because they were sinless—although God allowed them the capacity to sin because he gave them freedom of will. The plan was they would live forever in a perfect relationship with God, and in a perfect environment of God's own design. Then God's created beings made in his likeness sinned against their creator. When they sinned in the Garden of Eden one of the immediate consequences was separation from God (Genesis 2:17). Spiritual death came to God's creation. Their body did not immediately die, and their soul continued to live, but their spirit died. Death of the spirit was immediate when they sinned. They were instantly, spiritually separated from God. As a result, the Bible speaks of a person who is unsaved as being dead in trespasses and sin (Ephesians 2:1). When a person is saved he is spoken of as having passed from death unto life (John 5:24). John 3:16 also confirms the fact that when a person believes on the Lord Jesus Christ, he receives life (John 3:16).

The New Testament also describes the salvation of the body. This does not take place at the time that the spirit is saved, but at a later date. The body has been purchased and the price was the shed blood of the Lord Jesus Christ (1 Corinthians 6:19, 20). The down payment on this purchase has been made, but the body awaits its redemption (Ephesians 1:13, 14). While the body continues in this purchased yet unredeemed condition, it creates a conflict between the flesh and the spirit (Galatians 5:17–21). It is important to note that this conflict is possible only in Christians. The person whose spirit is not born from above (or renewed, regenerated, redeemed), cannot do anything to please God. His very nature leads him only and always into things contrary to the will of God. Name an act of benevolence. None will suffice to please God as a casual observer of the act, because it was not done first to honor God. Paul said in Romans 7:24, "Wretched man that I am! Who will deliver me from this body of death?" Here is the cry of a saved spirit in the unredeemed body calling for help and for deliverance. The question is logically asked, "When does salvation come to the body?" The body is not redeemed until the return of the Lord Jesus Christ (1 Corinthians 15:51–57). The bodies of both the redeemed and unredeemed who have died are currently in the grave. All bodies will be raised but, as we shall see later, will be raised at two different moments in time. The bodies of the redeemed will rise first and be made "incorruptible" (i.e., immortal). The redeemed who are living at the time of the return of the Lord will be raised into the air while at the same time their bodies will become immortal. Then and only then do the redeemed have the salvation of the body.

The New Testament also describes the salvation of the soul. The Bible's definition of the soul is similar to the English word "life" with all of its implications. For instance, Leviticus 17:11 says, "For the life of the flesh is in the blood: and I have given it to you upon the altar to make an atonement for your souls: for it is the blood that takes an atonement by the life (soul)." The word translated "life" in this verse is *nephesh* in the Hebrew. The Hebrew word for spirit is *ruach*. The literal translation, therefore, is "the soul is in the blood." Speaking of Jesus, Isaiah 53:12 says, he poured out his soul to death. The soul being in the blood is at once seen to animate the body and flesh. When a person has been redeemed through Christ—or as the Gospel of John describes it, born from above—he has the Spirit of God dwelling in him. When this happens, the body is then torn. The soul, in the natural state of man, pulls man toward the world and the things of the world. At the same time the born-again spirit of man pulls him toward God and the things of God. The soul in its natural, fallen state and the redeemed state of the spirit create the great conflict described so graphically by the apostle Paul in Galatians 5:16–26:

> But I say, walk by the Spirit, and you will not gratify the desires of the flesh. For the desires of the flesh are against the Spirit, and the desires of the Spirit are against the flesh, for these are opposed to each other, to keep you from doing the things you want to do. But if you are led by the Spirit, you are not under the law. Now the works of the flesh are evident: sexual immorality, impurity, sensuality, idolatry, sorcery, enmity, strife, jealousy, fits of anger, rivalries, dissensions, divisions, envy, drunkenness, orgies, and things like these. I warn you, as I warned you before, that those who do such things will not inherit the kingdom of God. But the fruit of the Spirit is love, joy, peace, patience, kindness, goodness, faithfulness, gentleness, self-control; against such things

there is no law. And those who belong to Christ Jesus have crucified the flesh with its passions and desires. If we live by the Spirit, let us also walk by the Spirit. Let us not become conceited, provoking one another, envying one another.

The only conclusion to which one can logically come to is that the loss which a person sustains is the soul; that is, to lose one's soul is to lose the rewards that will be brought by our Lord when he returns. These rewards are to be given to the faithful Christian and are to be enjoyed during the Millennial reign of Christ. The Millennial reign of Christ is a period of 1,000 years on earth commencing at the point of Christ's second appearing. Therefore, the future reward of the soul is something which is dependent upon man as he labors under the power of the Spirit of God. His spirit is secure in Christ, but his soul must continue to develop, day by day, in knowledge and truth.

It is very important to grasp this deeper understanding of the three principle parts of our being and the role the soul plays in our future life. Once saved the spirit is secure, but the struggles of our soul begin. Nevertheless, the Bible assures us that we are more than conquerors in Christ Jesus. We must overcome and conquer our soul because our appearance in the coming life is at stake.

CHAPTER 3

Preserving Your Soul

The Apostle Paul in the Epistle to the Hebrews reminds his readers that believers in Christ are to live by faith and in doing so "preserve their souls." In Hebrews 10:38–39 he says, "But my righteous one shall live by faith, and if he shrinks back, my soul has no pleasure in him. But we are not of those who shrink back and are destroyed, but of those who have faith and preserve their souls." The soul of every human being is perfectly content living in this dark, spiritual world dominated by evil. If we were never prompted by the Holy Spirit to accept God's gift of salvation, we would never choose of our own volition to live in the realm of existence dominated by faith. Despite being protected by the life boat of faith it is still possible to "shrink back"—as the Apostle Paul terms it—and fall under the devil's deceit. The Apostle Peter warns the church that the devil is an adversary who prowls around like a roaring lion, seeking someone to devour. (1 Peter 5:8). Believers must continuously work to rid their souls of the inclination toward evil. When the Apostle Paul, in Philippians 2:12, speaks of "working out your own salvation with fear and trembling" he is not speaking of continuing to fight to maintain salvation. Once received, salvation is secure. He is speaking instead about solidifying our reward in the future life; something that requires work and is not granted by grace.

In the context of the Protestant church, you are saved by grace, and any work on the believer's part is work that is required for reward in the life to come. And that is the context of Hebrews 10:38, 39. The King James translation of the Bible confusingly reads, "Now the just shall live by faith: but if *any man* draw back, my soul shall have no pleasure in him." The phrase "any man" is added to the King James; that is why it is printed in italics. It makes "any man" the subject of the verb "to draw back." But the subject should be the "just man." It is "if the *just man* draws back"—not *any man*. Be careful of the translation you are reading. It is the "righteous one" who must not shrink back. An unbeliever cannot draw back from living for the Lord, but a saved person can. An unbeliever cannot live for self and lose his rewards, but a saved person can. An unbeliever cannot appear at the judgment seat of Christ without any works of gold, silver or precious stones; suffer loss and be saved as though by fire—but a saved person can.

John MacArthur, of Grace to You radio ministry, pastor, and author of numerous books is reported to be an early advocate of the movement known as "Lordship Salvation." An otherwise sound preacher, he advocates that what you believe and do is directly related to maintaining your salvation. Here's one of the things he has said in his book *The Gospel According to Jesus*: "You must receive Jesus Christ for who He is, both Lord and Savior, to be truly saved." And regarding eternal security, he states this in his book *Saved Without a Doubt: Being Sure of Your Salvation*, "It should never be presented merely as a matter of being once saved, always saved—with no regard for what you believe or do. The writer of Hebrews 12:14 states frankly that only those who continue living holy lives will enter the Lord's presence. This is a classic example of what happens if you confuse soul and spirit, and the clear biblical distinction the Bible makes in this matter.

The shrinking back to destruction of which Hebrews 10:39 speaks is not to eternal damnation but is to the loss of the soul which is so plainly revealed in Matthew 16:24–27:

> Then Jesus told his disciples, "If anyone would come after me, let him deny himself and take up his cross and follow me. For whoever would save his life will lose it, but whoever loses his life for my sake will find it. For what will it profit a man if he gains the whole world and forfeits his life? Or what shall a man give in return for his life? For the Son of Man is going to come with his angels in the glory of his Father, and then he will repay each person according to what he has done. Truly, I say to you, there are some standing here who will not taste death until they see the Son of Man coming in his kingdom."

In the second appearing of Jesus Christ our Lord and Savior, when he comes for his own, those who have chosen in this life to lose their souls (or lives) for His sake shall receive rewards. But those who have chosen to save their lives, (or souls), for themselves in this life shall lose their rewards. The Christian cannot lose his salvation, but he can most assuredly lose his rewards. That is to say, salvation is given by grace (nothing you can do to earn it). Salvation is eternal. Reward is received when Christ returns. It is received because of your work for the Lord in this life. The saving of the soul is something future and is conditioned upon the behavior of the individual himself. That is where Lordship Salvation advocates get confused. Eternal life is the gift of God and can NEVER be lost or forfeited; but the saving of the soul is distinctly set forth in the Bible, not as a gift, but as a reward to be earned by diligence, faithfulness and obedience to His commands. Failure to distinguish between soul and spirit has caused many to err and make shipwreck of their faith—not that they are lost, but that they may experience the tragedy of having their spirit and body saved but their soul lost.

You might be asking yourself, "Are not the soul and the spirit the same? No, they are not. The soul is the natural life of the man—the self-life. It is the sum total of the experiences which pertain to the person himself; his own separate personality. It is the life the person lives daily after he is saved. He can live for the Lord or he can live for the world, the flesh and the devil. Such a life can result in gaining rewards or gathering losses. 1 Peter 1:5 reads, "who by God's power are being guarded through faith for a salvation ready to be revealed in the last time." 1 Peter1:9 reads, "obtaining the outcome of your faith, the salvation of your souls." The salvation to be revealed in the end time is that of the soul, unto rewards. 1 Peter 1:17 says, "And if you call on him as Father who judges impartially according to each one's deeds, conduct yourselves with fear throughout the time of your exile." The fear of the Lord qualifies and determines our walk. The Apostle Paul said, "Therefore, knowing the fear of the Lord, we persuade others." (2 Corinthians 5:11). The fear to which he is speaking is in regard to the judgment seat of Christ. Peter says, "Beloved, I urge you as sojourners and exiles to abstain from the passions of the flesh, which wage war against your soul. Keep your conduct among the Gentiles honorable, so that when they speak against you as evildoers, they may see your good deeds and glorify God on the day of visitation." (1 Peter 2:11, 12).

Consider what the Bible says about the awful plight of the following unfaithful servants. They are servants of the Lord and not lost people: One whose righteousness does not exceed that of the Pharisees—Matthew 5:20; one who was at the wedding feast but had no wedding garment—Matthew 22:1–14; the five who having oil in their lamps were careless and did not carry an extra supply—Matthew 25:1–13; the one who appeared at the judgment seat of Christ but had done nothing for the Lord—Matthew 25:14–30; that servant who knew his Master's will but did not do it—Luke 12:42–48; and, those who yield to works of the flesh instead of being led by the Spirit—Galatians 5:17–21.

Do not make the common mistake of confusing the biblical expressions the Kingdom of Heaven, the Kingdom of God, the Kingdom of His dear Son, the Kingdom of Light, and similar expressions with "eternal life," because they are different. In all but a few exceptions, all these expressions refer to and mean the Millennial reign of the

Lord Jesus Christ; and all the exhortations and warnings and promises printed above pertain to Christians who now, in this lifetime, are granted an opportunity to qualify for a place in the Kingdom by being faithful and obedient. It is sad today that the force of these warnings is taken away by preachers and teachers who simply misapply them. A wrong understanding encourages and promotes laxity of Christian life by teaching Christians to disregard the multiple warnings given by God. Here is a paraphrase of Hebrews 10:38–39: "For in a very little while, Christ will come swiftly; and when he comes those who have lived for him in this life shall receive their added blessing. But those believers who have shrunk back I will not be happy with them. We ought not to be shrinking back again toward destruction, but to a deeper working-out of our faith in Christ in order to receive a greater fulfillment...a greater reward, in the life to come."

In 1 Thessalonians 5:23, the Apostle Paul prays that the saints of Thessalonica might be wholly saved; that is, their spirits, their souls and their bodies. Hebrews 4:12 describes the dividing asunder of the soul and spirit by the Word of God. The salvation of the spirit takes place immediately and for eternity the moment an individual receives the Lord Jesus Christ as his Savior (John 3:36). To use the words of John Wesley, this verse emphasizes that belief produces present salvation for eternity. The body is not redeemed or saved until the resurrection and transition of the body. Romans 8:23 says, "And not only the creation, but we ourselves, who have the firstfruits of the Spirit, groan inwardly as we wait eagerly for adoption as sons, the redemption of our bodies."

The Salvation of the soul includes rewards for a life saved or lived in obedience unto and for the honor and glory of the Lord. That a "life" can be lost, though spirit and body are saved, is confirmed by the following Scriptures: 1 Corinthians 3:15, where a Christian is saved as through fire but suffers loss because his life was not lived unto the Lord; and, Revelation 16:15, which describes the possibility of a Christian losing his garments if he is not watchful in keeping his garments. To the contrary, our wedding garments—the robe of righteousness, which is by faith in the Lord Jesus Christ—can never be lost nor taken from us. We may also reference Revelation 3:11 which speaks of the possibility of a Christian losing his crown, and if there is no crown there can be no reigning with the Lord.; and, Matthew 25:28 which tells of the loss of money (the talent) by the one who did not use it and therefore does not enter into the joy of the Lord as he reigns. Notice in verse 14 of that same chapter that this one-talent servant is called "his own." In Luke 19:24 the servant of the Lord who did not use his money (mina) forfeited the money and therefore was not appointed to reign over any city or cities. The reigning over a city has nothing to do with salvation at all but with rewards for faithfulness.

Looking again to Hebrews 10:38–39, we note that the person under discussion is the just one (the believer). We also note that if the just one draws back (regresses), the Lord's soul has no pleasure in him. We further note in verse 39 that the drawing back on the part of the just one is unto destruction. Since it cannot be the destruction of the spirit and has nothing to do with the body, it must be the soul which is being described in these verses. In the closing part of verse 39 the just one can believe (be faithful) to the saving or salvation of his soul. A believer cannot draw back from salvation but the believer can draw back from the pilgrim life and live the carnal life as described by the Apostle Paul in 1 Corinthians 3:1–3; that is, he continues to be a babe in Christ all of his life.

> "But I, brothers, could not address you as spiritual people, but as people of the flesh, as infants in Christ. I fed you with milk, not solid food, for you were not ready for it. And even now you are not yet ready, for you are still of the flesh. For while there is jealousy and strife among you, are you not of the flesh and behaving only in a human way?"

The key expression of the Book of Hebrews is "Let us go on to perfection"; that is, let us go on to maturity, a full grown adult in Christ, not feeding continually on milk but going on to the meat of the Word. The meat of the Word in Hebrews is the truth and teaching pertaining to the kingdom and the possibility of Christians ruling and reigning with the Lord. The sincere milk of the Word has to do with the simple gospel message which is able to make one wise unto salvation; whereas the meat of the Word will enable a person to qualify for a place of sovereignty in the kingdom. Everywhere in the Bible that the salvation of the soul is mentioned it is referred to as a future event and is conditioned upon the life of the individual. For instance, in Matthew 16:24–27, a literal translation would be that whosoever "wills" to save his life shall lose it and whosoever "wills" to lose his life for Christ's sake shall find it. The saving of the life (soul) or the losing of the life (soul) is determined by the Christian's willing participation. In verse 24, the people being discussed are named by God as being His disciples. "If any disciples will come after Me..." As you read this entire passage you see that the result of the loss or saving of the soul has to do with the rewards mentioned in verse 27. The word translated "life" twice in verse 25 and "soul" twice in verse 26 is actually the same word in the Greek (psuche).

Eternal life is the gift of God and can never be lost, forfeited, given up, or taken from a person; whereas the saving of the soul is dependent on man himself. The salvation of the soul comes at the end of our life on earth, rather than the beginning; and one of the goals of faith in Jesus is the salvation of the soul or rewards. In 1 Peter 1:9 he writes of the "saving of the soul" to those who have already been born again. In the Book of James 1:21, he writes of the saving of the souls of those who have already been born again by the word of truth. The new birth—being born from above (i.e., regenerated), is a past experience for all who have believed on the Lord Jesus Christ; whereas the saving of the life or soul, which results in rewards, is a future experience which will be determined by the results of the judgment seat of Christ. In Philippians 2:12, Christians are urged to "work out your own salvation with fear and trembling." By so doing they will guarantee to themselves the receiving of rewards.

In 2 Peter 1:10, Christians are urged to give diligence to make their calling and election sure so that they will not stumble and lose their rewards but, according to verse 11, will have an abundant entrance into the everlasting kingdom of our Lord and Savior Jesus Christ. The salvation of the life (soul) of a Christian will guarantee such a place of sovereignty, honor, glory, with crowns and rewards in the kingdom of our Lord. The loss of one's life (soul) as a Christian will not result in banishment from heaven, but simply in relegating him to be a subject rather than a sovereign. My own personal conviction, born of study of the Bible, observation, and prayer is that the most dangerous teaching of too many Bible teachers is that Christians can live any way they want to and still rule and reign with the Lord. Consider these things. Ponder them and allow yourself to deepen your knowledge of the Bible. This is a subject of extreme importance to our life here on earth, and especially as our conduct now leads to greater fulfillment in the life to come.

CHAPTER 4

The Moment You Die

There is a very intriguing expression found in the Book of Revelation concerning the soul of man after death. The Apostle John, in Revelation 6:9–11, speaks of his vision of Christ on the Throne opening seven sealed scrolls. When he got to the fifth seal, John says, "I saw under the altar the souls of those who had been slain for the word of God and for the witness they had borne." John tells us that they speak. They cry aloud, "how long before you will judge and avenge our blood on those who dwell on the earth?" And then, we are told that these souls had a physical presence, because they where given a white robe and told to rest a little longer, until the number of their fellow servants and their brothers would be made complete. The intriguing expression I am referring to is, "I saw under the altar the souls." When was the last time you happened to see a soul? In this plane of life we do not see souls? We recognize that people have souls. We know a person's soul by his expressions, habits, and actions, but we cannot see the soul causing these things. Yet, after death the soul somehow becomes visible. It communicates. For the Apostle John, the appearance of these souls was below, not up. He said that he observed the souls, "under" the altar.

Theologians interpret the Book of Revelation in several different ways. For the purpose of this book we interpret it to be written for us to understand literally—with most of its content referring to still future events. That is not to say that there are not numerous figurative statements that require interpretation of its symbolism. Therefore, when the Apostle John says that he *saw* souls under the altar we assume that he actually visualized it and reported what he saw.

We have seen that the Bible regards man's *being* to be made of spirit, soul, and body; and that we are brought to salvation in Christ by our *spirit,* which is that portion of *being* that has a connection to God. The Bible says we were made in his "image (likeness)." That image must be a spiritual image—since God is himself "spirit." Our *soul,* on the other hand, is what we might call our consciousness; our personality and the sum total of our experiences and thinking. God works in our *spirit* to incline us toward Christ; or what is sometimes referred to as the "Call of Christ." Our *spirit* begins the work of bringing our *soul* into a relationship with our spirit's new found inclination toward God. That process of uniting spirit and soul, inclining our thoughts toward a relationship with Christ, and rejecting the world's desire for sin and its pleasures is a life-long process. But, for some, the "prompting of the spirit" is something that the soul habitually rejects. Even though Christ's atoning death is sufficient for all to receive by the reasoning of the soul, some will reject God's merciful call. Yet, no matter if you are saved by the atoning work of Christ on the Cross, or reject the call to salvation, the body continues to decay. It wears out and dies.

It is at the moment of death that something profound happens regarding the spirit, soul, and body. The moment you take your last breath, each goes through a transformation. For now, I would like to concentrate our attention primarily on our *soul* and answer the question, "What happens to our soul at the moment of death?" If we were to take the time to thoroughly go through the Bible, we would discover that it reveals a number of things related to the soul. One of the key things the Bible says about the soul is: Death does *not* end the existence of the soul. We are told that in the afterlife, souls continue to exist and become visible. That is to say, you can see personality. Souls are conscious. They can remember the past. And at death our soul and spirit remain connected (as in life) to focus our attention toward Christ. At the moment of death our body begins to return to dust. It remains in this state in the ground for a period of time until Christ returns to claim his Church and give to each a new physical form—one which is eternal and without blemish or defect.

While there are many Bible references pertaining to this subject, one in particular can provide us with great value regarding the afterlife and the soul. In Luke 16:19–31 we have the experience of the rich man, Lazarus and Abraham. All three are seen in their *soul* experience. Here is what Luke says:

> There was a rich man who was clothed in
> purple and fine linen and who feasted sump-
> tuously every day. And at his gate was laid
> a poor man named Lazarus, covered with

sores, who desired to be fed with what fell from the rich man's table. Moreover, even the dogs came and licked his sores. The poor man died and was carried by the angels to Abraham's side. The rich man also died and was buried, and in Sheol, being in torment, he lifted up his eyes and saw Abraham far off and Lazarus at his side. And he called out, "Father Abraham, have mercy on me, and send Lazarus to dip the end of his finger in water and cool my tongue, for I am in anguish in this flame." But Abraham said, "Child, remember that you in your lifetime received your good things, and Lazarus in like manner bad things; but now he is comforted here, and you are in anguish. And besides all this, between us and you a great chasm has been fixed, in order that those who would pass from here to you may not be able, and none may cross from there to us." And he said, "Then I beg you, father, to send him to my father's house—for I have five brothers—so that he may warn them, lest they also come into this place of torment." But Abraham said, "They have Moses and the Prophets; let them hear them." And he said, "No, father Abraham, but if someone goes to them from the dead, they will repent." He said to him, "If they do not hear Moses and the Prophets, neither will they be convinced if someone should rise from the dead."

Notice that the rich man's *soul* has a form. He can feel the flames. He wants water to cool his tongue. And notice that Lazarus has fingers which the rich man thinks could touch his lips with water. Abraham, Lazarus and the rich man all have eyes, ears, voices, because they see, hear and speak. We conclude that souls are tangible, possessing form and characteristics which were theirs before death. And we recall that Christ with his appearing after his death was able to be seen by his disciples but could also enter rooms through locked doors—a kind of foreshadowing of what is contained in this story. Lazarus is dead, but you can see his soul. It has tangible characteristics of human form.

At the moment of death the soul instantaneously travels to a temporary resting place, and there it remains until Christ's planned appearing in the air. That appearing is known in the Bible as the Rapture. The Bible refers to this temporary place as *Sheol*—or, the "place of departed souls." This is the place where the souls of the righteous and the wicked go at their departure from the body. The popular theological answer is, the soul of the righteous goes to heaven, and the soul of the wicked (or unrighteous, if you prefer) immediately goes to hell. For the Catholic adherent, so long as you are a member in good standing (i.e., take the sacraments, confess your sins, do good works), you have a direct path to heaven—but first, with a stop for an unspecified length of time in a temporary holding place called Purgatory.

Be careful. If each soul at death goes at once (as many people think), to receive his respective reward or punishment, why is there need for a future "judgment" that is described in the New Testament? For example, 2 Corinthians 5:10 says, "For we must all appear before the judgment seat of Christ, so that each one may receive what is due for what he has done in the body, whether good or evil." In other words, if, as is commonly said, the soul is judged at death, what is the need of the *second judgment* referred to in the Bible as the White Throne of Judgment? If you take that view—that we are immediately judged at death and go to heaven or hell—it is no wonder that the notion of the Millennium is rejected. (The Millennium being the thousand years that Christ will reign on earth, as described in Revelation, chapter 20). If there is a future judgment—and the Bible says there is—think of it, what pleasure would there be in returning to the cold earth to be judged after an experience of the brightness in the presence of God in heaven? Also, if the disembodied spirit can enter at once into the full happiness of heaven, why then would it need to be reunited with a new body? The point is this, one mistaken notion of scripture affects another, because there is a relationship in the many parts of understanding the future life. The wrenching away of one part disturbs the many other parts.

Take for example Christ's soul. What became of Christ's soul after death? We say in the Apostles Creed—"He descended into hell, and on the third day he rose again from the dead..." And when we question "what is meant here of hell" the usual reply is that it signifies the eternal place of departed *spirits*. But this supports the theory that the departed go immediately to either hell or heaven. It's confusing, to say the least. All of this confusion is why many are content to think that we cannot really know anything about the state of death. We believe it must remain a mystery. Who can know? But, is that a fair question? The answer is, no. We can know, because the Bible unlocks the key to this mystery. But it must be examined with care. One such examination involves the word *Sheol* which in the Hebrew always and only meant "the place of the dead." English translations typically render the word "the grave," and sometimes by the word "hell"; but the word never has that as its first meaning. There is another term altogether different to express the grave, or the place of the body's resting place. It is the word *taphos* in the Greek, *geber* in the Hebrew.

In the Bible, *Sheol* always signifies the resting place of the *soul*. In the early Greek translation known as the Septuagint, the translators invariably render the word Sheol as *Hades*, and that term we accept as unerringly used by the writers of the New Testament the way it was intended to be interpreted. Therefore, whether you read the word Sheol, or Hades, it has the same meaning.

A further investigation of the story of Lazarus and the rich man in Luke, chapter 16, reveals that Sheol is a temporary receptacle for the dead, and it is divided into two portions—one for the righteous, and one for the wicked. In the story this division becomes clear. We read of a great divide between the two men. Nevertheless, some want to say that this story is just a parable—its not a real story. But, if that is accurate, if it is only a fictitious story, it is the only parable in which the Lord uses a person's name. Typically, Jesus starts his parables with something like, "There was a certain man" with no mention of specific names. Here in this parable we not only have a name, but the story goes deeper and mentions that the rich man has "five brothers"; meaning, a very specific family. Abraham's name is also mentioned.

Sheol is a temporary holding place until the Lord's return. It holds both the saved and the unsaved. We have previously mentioned that there is a tangible form to our soul upon death. In Sheol the soul can be seen. The body turns to dust in the ground, but the soul immediately enters Sheol. In between the time that we are absent from this present body and the time we enter our eternal heavenly home, our souls possess a tangible form comparable to that of the souls John is speaking of in Revelation 6: "I saw under the altar the souls of those who had been slain for the word of God and for the witness they had borne." For the unjust, the unrighteous, the wicked, the unsaved (as they are referred to), Sheol is a place of torment. But it is not the torment that will imprison them for eternity. For these souls, Sheol is a place of fire, but not the fire they will experience when they are forcibly removed from Sheol by the angels and sent into *Gehenna* (i.e., eternal hell). The Book of Jude says, "Sodom and Gomorrah, and the cities about them, in like manner giving themselves over to fornication, and going after strange flesh, are set forth for an example, suffering the vengeance of eternal fire." The same is evident from the parable of the rich man and Lazarus, "I am tormented in this flame," says the rich man. Worse yet, when the unsaved finally arrive in Gehenna (Hell), they will discover degrees of torment—some worse than others. Jesus alludes to this in Matthew 10:15 when he said, "Truly, I say to you, it will be more bearable on the day of judgment for the land of Sodom and Gomorrah than for that town."

Sheol is constantly and clearly distinguished in the New

Testament. But this distinction is lost to the English reader, because our translators have written Sheol and Gehenna as the same word. But the New Testament, in its original language, always makes this difference—that Sheol (or Hades as it is known in the Greek) is the present place of the dead. Gehenna is the future and eternal place of the wicked dead, after the second resurrection and judgment which is to take place at the end of the thousand year reign of Christ upon the earth.

Gehenna is not mentioned in many places in the Bible; but where it is, its punishment is spoken of as eternal. Matthew 5:22 says, "...and whoever says, 'You fool!' will be liable to the hell of fire." (literally, "the *Gehenna* of fire"). Matthew 5:29, 30 says, "If your right eye causes you to sin, tear it out and throw it away. For it is better that you lose one of your members than that your whole body be thrown into hell (i.e., Geheena). And if your right hand causes you to sin, cut it off and throw it away. For it is better that you lose one of your members than that your whole body go into hell." (i.e., Gehenna). Matthew 10:28 states, "And do not fear those who kill the body but cannot kill the soul. Rather fear him who can destroy both soul and body in hell." (i.e., Gehenna).

Less is said of the righteous soul in the Bible, but there is enough for us to sketch its general state of thought and expectation. The Apostle Paul informs his readers concerning what he calls Paradise (i.e., Sheol), that "he heard things that cannot be told, which man may not utter." (2 Corinthians 12:4). So unutterable were the joys, so incapable of being comprehended by man in the flesh, that the Apostle Paul was overwhelmed as to whether he was in the body or not. He thought he must have been dreaming. So deep was the impression of the peace that he enjoyed that he had a desire "to depart, and be with Christ, which is far better."

There are many who mistakenly object to the concept of Sheol because they incorrectly think it is an undesirable place for the righteous. They think it is dark and foreboding like the grave. But it is not. It is far from it. The Apostle Paul says otherwise. The misperception stems from a prejudice which has arisen out of learning from the systems of man, rather than the declaration of the Word of God. Even so, the "place" does not provide absolute fulfillment for the believer. It will be sufficient for him that he is where God places him. It is enough that in Paradise (Sheol) there is peace and calm and joy, such as earth cannot bestow. It is enough that Christ is present with us, in a greater degree than we discover here on earth. The Lord himself passed through the depths of Sheol that he might, as the Bible says, "be lord both of the dead and the living"; and that even there he may visit believers with his Spirit.

And it appears that even there the righteous are engaged in praise. We discover this at the opening of the "book with seven seals," in Revelation 5:13, which reads: "And I heard every creature in heaven and on earth and UNDER THE EARTH and in the sea, and all that is in them, saying, 'To him who sits on the throne and to the Lamb be blessing and honor and glory and might forever and ever!'" The phrase "under the earth" cannot mean *evil spirits*, because they would not glorify and praise Christ; nor can they be the wicked souls of men in *Sheol*, for the same reason. Therefore, they are the souls of the righteous, whose present habitation is described as being under the earth. Similarly we have the passages of Philippians 2:9, 10 which read, "Therefore God has highly exalted him and bestowed on him the name that is above every name, so that at the name of Jesus every knee should bow, in heaven and on earth and UNDER THE EARTH."

We discover, however, from other passages, that their peace, though great, and their happiness, though considerable, is still not complete and final. We learn from Revelation 6: 9–11, that there is a state of waiting and a longing desire for Christ's return, as the day of their complete joy—"When he opened the fifth seal, I saw under the altar the souls of those who had been slain for the word of God and for the witness they had borne. They cried out with a loud voice, 'O Sovereign Lord, holy and true, *how long* before you will judge and avenge our blood on those who dwell on the earth?' Then they were each given a white robe and told to *rest a little longer*, until the number of their fellow servants and their brothers should be complete, who were to be killed as they themselves had been." Notice again, John said "I SAW the souls." He could see them. They had a form, a type of tangible image that made them visible, and they were anxiously awaiting Christ's appearing.

In 1 Thessalonians 4:16, there is an unusual description of Christ's actions concerning the dead rising. It reads, "For the Lord himself will descend from heaven with a cry of command, with the voice of an archangel, and with the sound of the trumpet of God. And the dead in Christ will rise first." Why should the dead in Christ rise first? Why not everyone rise to meet Christ in the air—both living and dead—at the same time? The dead have a preferred position over that of the living. It is likely because those who are already dead have souls that are residing in Sheol and have experienced a form of worship with Christ. They are not worshiping to the fullest extent of their ability or desire. That will not happen until their soul is reunited with their new, immortal body. In the meantime, they long for greater worship because they already have a concept of the joy of deeper worship; whereas those of us who are still alive have only a vague concept of what worship is like. Therefore, in God's mercy, those souls who have already experienced intimate worship with the Lord and long for greater worship are granted the privilege of receiving their immortal bodies first.

Not every soul in Sheol longs for worship. Some are focused on their torment. Jakob Martini (1570–1649), a seventeenth-century German theologian wrote this: "It is thus evident that of old there were two different places of abode for souls; one for the good, and the other for the evil; yet both the one and the other is called Sheol. The place of the ungodly, however, is called 'the Lowest Sheol,' but the place of the just 'the Upper Sheol.'" In the Book of Ecclesiastes 1:7 we read. "All streams run to the sea, but the sea is not full; to the place where the streams flow, there they flow again." That is to say, all the dead go into Sheol (Hades) only, yet Sheol is never full. Proverbs 27:20 also reads, "Sheol is never full." Nathan said the same thing to King David. In 2 Samuel 12:13 we read, "David said to Nathan, 'I have sinned against the LORD.' And Nathan said to David, 'The LORD also has put away your sin; you shall not die.'" What is implied is, "you will not descend to the lowest depth of Sheol; you will not experience separation from God." Psalm 86:13 reads, "For great is your steadfast love toward me; you have delivered my soul from the *depths* of Sheol (or, literally, the "lowest" Sheol)." Christ has rescued us from entering into that lowest depth. It is a free gift of God.

CHAPTER 5

The Resurrection of Your Body

In the previous chapter we discussed what happens to the soul and spirit at the moment of death. In this chapter we want to consider the body and the transformation that takes place after death. A portion of Scripture that helps to explain how and when the soul and body are reunited after death is given to us by Jesus in the Gospel of Mark, 9:9, 10. The scene is of Jesus and several of his disciples descending from the top of a mountain. The verses read, "And as they were coming down the mountain, he (Jesus) charged them to tell no one what they had seen, until the Son of Man had *risen from the dead.* So they kept the matter to themselves, questioning what this *rising from the dead* might mean." To help place this twice-repeated phrase "rising from the dead" in context we need to once again consider the "being" of man and answer what constitutes man in a divine sense of being. The answer is man is made-up of soul, spirit, and body. What was Jesus saying in verses 9 about rising from the dead that caused the disciples to question among themselves what the phrase might mean?

We first need to clean-up and correct the English translation of the Greek words used in these two verses. In the Greek (the original language of the verses) the phrase translated "raised from the dead is "*tow ek nekron anestemi.*" The word *ek* means "out of." Christ was actually saying he would rise from "out of" the dead, not "with" the dead. This special kind of rising from among the dead, was to be kept a secret. Whenever Jesus told a disciple to keep something a secret it was because the Jewish people would not as yet been able to understand what would soon be taking place after his death.

Recall from the previous chapter that at the moment of death our soul and spirit instantly relocate to Sheol—that temporary holding place for both the righteous and the unrighteous. John experienced a vision of this, when he said in the Book of Revelation, chapter 6, "I saw the souls under the altar." These were the righteous souls in Sheol; people visible to his eyes. But in Sheol there are two groups of people: the righteous and the unrighteous, those who died saved by faith, and those who died having rejected the offer of salvation. These two groups are separated by a great gulf which cannot be crossed. Jesus described the location of the righteous as *Paradise*. He said to the thief hanging next to him on the cross, "today you will be with me in *Paradise.*" That expression could not mean Heaven, because the Bible speaks of Jesus' soul and spirit having "descended" into Sheol at the moment of death. Isaiah chapter 61 describes why Christ descended into Sheol. It says that Christ would, "proclaim liberty to the captives, and the opening of the prison to those who are bound." The verse refers to the righteous being held in Sheol who were now declared to be there only temporarily, because Jesus was in the process of setting them free to move on to eternity with him—something Revelation chapter 6 describes as the righteous longing to experience.

But the action concerning the *body* and what takes place after death is not quite as straight forward as that of our soul and spirit. There is a progression in the unfolding of information about the "rising of the body." Does the body rise and move-on like the soul and spirit at the moment of death? If not, how and when is it resurrected? The Bible speaks of the body returning to the earth as dust, but it never says it remains in that condition. What happens to the body and what does it mean when the Bible speaks of "the resurrection of the dead?" One thing is certain, that when the Bible speaks of "resurrection" it is speaking of the body alone, and not the soul or spirit. There is a progression in the teaching of the Word of God relative to "resurrection." Prior to the resurrection of Christ there was mention only of the resurrection *of* the dead. In the Greek it is, "*anastaseos tow nekron*," translated "and of resurrection of dead ones." In Hebrews 6:1, 2 we read, "Therefore let us leave the elementary doctrine of Christ and go on to maturity, not laying again a foundation of repentance from dead works and of faith toward God, and of instruction about washings, the laying on of hands, the resurrection of the dead, and eternal judgment." According to the author of Hebrews, this is elementary teaching—important but elementary. The author is saying, "we need to advance beyond the basic understanding of the *resurrection of the dead*." From the very beginning of the church, when Creeds were formed by the church to bring attention to the orthodox (meaning the "center line") teachings of the church, the Apostles Creed stated, in part: "...I believe in the Holy Ghost, the holy catholic church, the communion of saints, the forgiveness of sins, the resurrection of the body, and the life everlasting." The resurrection of the body was a basic, accepted teaching of the church, but it was considered by the Apostle Paul to be an elementary teaching. Believers should advance beyond the elementary teaching of the doctrine.

In the account of the Mount of Transfiguration, as the Lord was coming down from the mountain, he charged Peter, James and John (who were on the mountain with him), not to mention the experience until he, Christ, had risen "out from among the dead." These disciples who had heard only of the resurrection *of* the dead could not understand what the Lord meant by the expression "the rising from *among* (or "out of") the dead." In the Greek it is literally translated: "raised out from among the dead ones"; that is to say, "from among the dead being resurrected, to be raised apart from those dead." The Apostle Paul in his letter to the Philippians describes his sole-ambition, the burning desire of his heart, his obsession, and calls it "the out-resurrection" (Philippians 3:11). In the Greek the expression is: "*ek-anastasin ten ek nekros.*" The literal translation is: "the out-resurrection from among those who have been raised from among the dead ones." What the Apostle Paul meant was that he was assured of rising from the dead when he died; but he was not sure of a further rising or selection after he was raised from among the dead, because there was a further rising, another rising, that was dependent upon something other than faith. It was dependent upon faithfulness, obedience, and it had to be attained, earned, merited, won as a "prize." So the Apostle Paul said, "this one thing I do." He would do all in his power to win the prize of the "out-calling" from among those raised from among the dead ones and thereby rule and reign with our Lord in his coming kingdom—the thousand year reign, or Millennial reign, as Scripture refers to it.

When the Bible speaks of the dead rising, it is speaking of the body rising. The Bible provides us with a progression on this subject of the dead rising: First, all the dead will be raised. Second, the dead in Christ will be raised from among the unrighteous dead ones before the Tribulation begins. The Old Testament saints will be raised at the end of the Tribulation, and the rest of the dead will not be raised for a thousand years. The following are Scripture references on the subject.

> 1 Thessalonians 4:13–17: "But we do not want you to be uninformed, brothers, about those who are asleep, that you may not grieve as others do who have no hope. For since we believe that Jesus died and rose again, even so, through Jesus, God will bring with him those who have fallen asleep. For this we declare to you by a word from the Lord, that we who are alive, who are left until the coming of the Lord, will not precede those who have fallen asleep. For the Lord himself will descend from heaven with a cry of command, with the voice of an archangel, and with the sound of the trumpet of God. And the dead in Christ will rise first. Then

we who are alive, who are left, will be caught up together with them in the clouds to meet the Lord in the air, and so we will always be with the Lord."

Daniel 12:1, 2: "At that time shall arise Michael, the great prince who has charge of your people. And there shall be a time of trouble, such as never has been since there was a nation till that time. But at that time your people shall be delivered, everyone whose name shall be found written in the book. And many of those who sleep in the dust of the earth shall awake, some to everlasting life, and some to shame and everlasting contempt."

Revelation 20:4–6: "Then I saw thrones, and seated on them were those to whom the authority to judge was committed. Also I saw the souls of those who had been beheaded for the testimony of Jesus and for the word of God, and who had not worshiped the beast or its image and had not received its mark on their foreheads or their hands. They came to life and reigned with Christ for a thousand years. The rest of the dead did not come to life until the thousand years were ended. This is the first resurrection. Blessed and holy is the one who shares in the first resurrection! Over such the second death has no power, but they will be priests of God and of Christ, and they will reign with him for a thousand years."

The third aspect mentioned in Scripture relating to the dead rising concerns the Rapture. After the resurrection of the Christians, described as the Rapture, there is an appearing before the judgment seat of Christ. This is a further rising, or selection, based not on faith in Christ, but on works *for* Christ. Possession of the wedding garment (as described in Jesus' parable) which depicts the privilege as well as responsibility of reigning with Christ in the Millennial reign. All Christians will be raised bodily from among the dead, *but* only those who are further selected will receive rewards and reign with Him.

Throughout the Old Testament there is the teaching of a *general* resurrection. The truth of several resurrections did not come to light until the experience of our Lord on the Mount of Transfiguration. In Mark 9:9 the Lord speaks of the Son of man rising from among the dead. Verse 10 reveals that the disciples did not know what He meant when He spoke of "rising from *among* the dead." Recall that in Hebrews 6:2 the resurrection of the dead is spoken of as one of the principles of the doctrine of Christ from which they were to go on to perfection—to expand knowledge. And perfection, so far as the doctrine of the resurrection is concerned, is grasping the truth of several resurrections rather than believing in just one general resurrection.

In the Merriam-Webster dictionary the word *resurrection* is defined as "a resumption of vigor; restoration; revival, which means to live again." Man is spirit, soul, and body.

When a person dies only his body dies; therefore, all that can live again or be resurrected is the body of the one who dies. In Job 14:14, the question is asked, "If a man die, shall he live again?" Technically speaking, this means if a man ceases to have a physical existence of flesh and bones, will he in the life to come, have a physical existence of flesh and bones? That question is answered in Job 19:25–27. Job, through the Spirit of God, says that though he dies and the worms eat his body, yet in his flesh shall he see God, and he will see him with his own physical eyes. In order for Job to do this, his body must come back from the dust and exist again in flesh and bones. The present body of man is called a *natural body* because it is animated by the soul. The resurrection body of man will be a *spiritual* body, that is, a body of flesh and bones animated by the Holy Spirit. 1 Corinthians 15:50 tells us that flesh and blood cannot inherit the kingdom of God; but Scripture is consistent in teaching that flesh and *bones* are to inherit the kingdom of God. Blood is corruptible and cannot enter into the kingdom of God, but the bodies of resurrected flesh and *bones*, given life through the Holy Spirit, will enter into the kingdom of God.

The entire 15th chapter of 1 Corinthians sets forth the fundamental truth that the bodily resurrection of Christ is the foundation stone of Christianity. The Apostle Paul said that without the resurrection of Christ's body there is no resurrection of the body for us. Because Christ's body of flesh and bones arose from the dead, so too shall all mankind arise from the dead in their bodies of flesh and bones. This is what 1 Corinthians 15:20–23 says: "But in fact Christ has been raised from the dead, the firstfruits of those who have fallen asleep. For as by a man came death, by a man has come also the resurrection of the dead. For as in Adam all die, so also in Christ shall all be made alive. But each in his own order: Christ the firstfruits, then at his coming those who belong to Christ." Now, there are some who choose not to believe in the physical resurrection of the dead. But that is based upon the pagan philosophy that matter is evil, only spirit is good. There was a poll taken of clergy in the Church of England which found that one-third doubt or disbelieve in the physical resurrection of Christ, and only half are convinced of the truth of the Virgin birth. What's worse, only half believe that faith in Christ is the only route to salvation.

Remember that there is a progression in the Word of God from a general teaching about the resurrection of the body to a more specific doctrine. When the Bible mentions resurrection it means the resurrection of the physical body of one who was alive but has died. Resurrection does not apply to soul or spirit since neither dies. Also remember that death is not a mystery. We should not fear death because when you take your last breath you will immediately be in Christ's presence—your soul and spirit intact forming a physical presence. You will speak, and feel; you will immediately recognize Christ, but you will long for his second appearing in order to rescue you from Sheol and subsequently move you into a far greater joy and union with your new, eternal body. All of this, of course, assumes you to be a Christian. It assumes that you have not taken your last breath prior to realizing that you are a sinner in need of forgiveness, repented of your inherited sin, accepted that Christ died and was resurrected from the dead to eternally cleanse you of that original sin, and acknowledged that Christ is the only means by which God can forgive your sins which separate you from acceptance into his presence. That is the picture the Bible paints for the person who dies in Christ (i.e., who has received the gift of eternal life in this life, who has surrendered his life to Christ, by repenting of his sins and desiring to let his spirit guide his soul into a deeper love for Christ).

But there's another picture altogether of the soul who goes into eternity while still denying Christ as his lord and savior. In the moment of death, that soul immediately feels the torment of fire and longs for relief. But it only gets worse. It's a dangerous game we play in this life, ignoring the Bible's clear teachings of death and beyond. It's dangerous because it has eternal consequence.

CHAPTER 6

Your Special Resurrection

We have previously noted that the resurrection pertains to the "body" and not to the soul or spirit. Your soul and spirit cannot die, only the body can die, and therefore, it is only the body that needs to be "resurrected." The body will be resurrected because Christ became our example in resurrection. Because Christ died, was buried, and rose again in bodily form we can have the confidence that he is our example. As the Apostle Paul notes in 1 Corinthians chapter 15, Christ is the firstfruit of the harvest to come (borrowing from the Old Testament description of renewal). We also previously noted that the Apostle Paul speaks of the resurrection as one of the fundamental doctrines of the church, and that it is an elementary teaching that needs to be understood in an expanding way—that is to say, there is more to be understood; deeper meaning. Jesus says as much in the verses concerning the event on the Mount of Transfiguration. He said that he will be raised "from out *from among* the dead." But he tells them not to tell anyone, because the Jews would not yet understand what it meant. We are told that the disciples were perplexed by what he meant. They knew about a general resurrection that was to take place pertaining to ALL the dead. Martha says as much when she is speaking to Jesus about her brother's death. In the Gospel of John 11:23, 24 there is a conversation between Jesus and Martha: "Jesus said to her, 'Your brother will rise again.' Martha said to him, 'I know that he will rise again in the resurrection on the *last day.*'" That is what the disciples also believed; that there was to be a "general resurrection" for *everyone* on the last day—the day in which all will be judged, and then the earth destroyed and a new heaven and earth created with God himself on the throne.

Now Jesus was introducing a "new" understanding of the doctrine concerning resurrection. Paul said Christians need to advance in their understanding of the resurrection. In the general resurrection there was no apparent distinction between the saved and the lost. All will be resurrected in the general resurrection that Martha was referring to. But, according to Jesus, there was now to be understood a *selective* resurrection, in addition to a general resurrection on the "last day." In Jesus' advanced teaching, some would be raised and others left in the graves.

The teaching of a resurrection from "among" the dead is introduced to the disciples with the experiences on the Mount of Transfiguration. In the Gospel of Mark 9:9 Jesus speaks of the Son of man to be raised from "among"the dead. This was so contrary to the thinking of the apostles that in verse 10 the disciples continued to discuss possible meanings of the Lord's statement, "rise from among the dead." In the general resurrection from the dead, which takes place (as Martha described it), on the "last day," all the bodies of the unsaved will rise to be judged. Everyone, saved and lost, will be judged on that last day. It will be the last act of Christ before the earth is destroyed and remade.

The Apostle Paul gives us a glimpse into the special resurrection spoken of by Jesus. He says in Philippians 3:11, "that by any means possible I may attain to the *out*-resurrection from the dead." Translators typically use the word "resurrection." But this word intentionally has a prefix added to it by the Apostle Paul; thus changing the meaning. Here Paul uses a word for resurrection that is not used any other time in the entire Bible; only here in this one place. The immediate context of this particular resurrection is that Paul knows with assurance that he will stand with those who will be raised from the dead to stand in judgment at that resurrection on the "last day"—which the Bible refers to it as the *White Throne of Judgment*. But he is looking forward to a further separation "from among" the risen saints, which he calls the *out*-resurrection. This *out*-resurrection is the prize which Paul mentions in verse 14; a prize for which he is working toward and can only "hope" to receive. He has no sense of it being a guarantee for him. It is a prize dependent upon his faithfulness as a Christian. And only Christ can unbiasedly judge and recompense. The Book of Revelation 20:6 says, "Blessed and holy is the one who shares in the first resurrection. Over such the second death has no power, but they will be priests of God and of Christ, and they will reign with him for a thousand years." That is the "selective resurrection." That is the resurrection which Paul hopes to attain to, the one in which he has no self-assurance. What he knows is that if he can attain to this special resurrection (the *out*-resurrection), he will with certainty avoid the "second death."

What is the second death? Revelation 21:8 describes it this way: "...their portion [those who are faithless] will be in the lake that burns with fire and sulfur, which is the second death." The second death is eternity in Hell, and the casting into it occurs after that final judgment (the White Throne of Judgment), to be administered on the "last day." In contrast, who will attain to this special resurrection? Luke describes it as the "resurrection of the just." He says in the Gospel of Luke 14:13, 14, "But when you give a feast, invite the poor, the crippled, the lame, the blind, and you will be blessed, because they cannot repay you. You will be repaid at the resurrection of the just." We discover that there are two resurrections—one for the resurrection of only the righteous, and a final resurrection involving all the unjust (or ungodly). The Gospel of Luke, in 20:34–36, further says: And Jesus said to them, "The sons of this age marry and are given in marriage, but those who are considered worthy to attain to that age and to the resurrection from the dead [actually "from *among* the dead"] neither marry nor are given in marriage, for they cannot die anymore, because they are equal to angels and are sons of God, being sons of the resurrection." This resurrection pertains to only the righteous since they are referred to as "sons of God." And they alone will be chosen to participate in reigning with Christ in "that age" to come; meaning, the thousand year reign on earth prior to the final judgment on the last day. But when does this special resurrection take place? It takes place prior to what is known as the Tribulation which is described in 1 Thessalonians 4:16, 17: "For the Lord himself will descend from heaven with a cry of command, with the voice of an archangel, and with the sound of the trumpet of God. And the dead in Christ will rise first. Then we who are alive, who are left, will be caught up together with them in the clouds to meet the Lord in the air, and so we will always be with the Lord."

The following is the summation of the Bible doctrine of resurrection: 1. There was revealed first to the people of God that there would be a resurrection OF the dead (John 11:24). 2. Christ revealed that there would be a resurrection FROM AMONG the dead (Mark 9:9,10; 1 Thessalonians 4:16; Revelation 20:5). 3. The Holy Spirit revealed to the Apostle Paul that there would be an OUT-resurrection FROM AMONG those who would be raised FROM AMONG the dead (Philippians 3:11). There is for every Christian the privilege and opportunity to strive, as did the Apostle Paul, to attain to the OUT-resurrection.

The gospel message is that Jesus died for our sins, was buried and rose again the third day according to the Scriptures. When an apostle was needed to be chosen to take the place of Judas they said, "One must be ordained to be a witness with us of His resurrection." On the day of Pentecost Peter, preaching to the multitude, spoke of this resurrection of the Lord Jesus Christ in the flesh. Peter and John were taken before the council and tried because they taught the people and preached the resurrection from the dead. When they were set free it was with great power that they gave witness of the resurrection of the Lord Jesus Christ; and the Bible says that great grace was upon them all. At Athens Paul preached that Jesus himself was raised from the dead and they mocked and laughed at this teaching and preaching of the resurrection of the dead. They said, "We will hear you again on this matter." Paul also stood before the council of the Pharisees and Sadducees and said, "Concerning the resurrection of the dead I am called in question." And in 1 Corinthians, chapter 15 Paul said, "And if Christ has not been raised, then our preaching is in vain and your faith is in vain." There were those at Corinth who believed in the resurrection of Jesus but denied the ascension of His body into heaven. They denied a future resurrection. But remember, Paul and the other apostles when speaking of the resurrection do not speak of the immortality of the *soul*. The soul is not mortal; the spirit is not mortal. Neither the soul nor the spirit is subject to death; only the body is mortal and only the body can be given immortality. Therefore, it is specifically the body that is central to the resurrection. It is in the resurrection that the body is reunited with the soul and spirit.

God's testimony to us is that the whole man—spirit, soul, and body—will be restored. Remember that when God created Adam in the garden of Eden—spirit, soul, and body—Adam was to eat of the tree of life and be preserved eternally in that spirit, soul, and body. That was God's original plan and purpose and that purpose has not been changed. The redemption of God includes the body, includes the soul, and includes the spirit; and for that Paul prayed in 1 Thessalonians 5:23, "Now may the God of peace himself sanctify you completely, and may your whole spirit and soul and body be kept blameless at the coming of our Lord Jesus Christ." Consider the Lord Jesus Christ when he died. He yielded his spirit to God the Father; his body went into the tomb and his soul went down into Sheol. In the death of the Lord Jesus Christ man's three component parts—spirit, soul, and body—were separated and went into three different places. The resurrection of the Lord Jesus Christ involved the bringing back of the spirit, the bringing back of the soul, and covering them with a new immortal body which is to be raised from the dead. And when we speak of the resurrection, that is what we mean: The body that is given back to earth is left in the dust; a new immortal body is to be raised up and is united one day with the soul, and spirit.

The Apostle Paul is contending that if he preaches that Christ rose from the dead, how can anybody say then that there is no resurrection of the dead, because if there is no resurrection of the dead, then Christ did not rise from the dead; and if Christ did not rise from the dead, he is still in the tomb. But we know that his tomb is an empty tomb. The greatest testimony to the resurrection of the Lord Jesus Christ is the empty tomb. The Word of God says that if you will confess with your mouth that Jesus is the Lord and believe in your heart that God has raised Him from the dead, you shall be saved. We are told that unless you believe that Jesus Christ has come in the flesh, and unless you believe that Jesus Christ is coming again in the flesh, you are of the spirit of the antichrist. The Apostle Paul says, "If Christ did not rise from the dead, I am a false witness, I am preaching falsehoods, I am preaching lies, I am misrepresenting God's truth to you because I have testified of God that He raised up Christ from the dead." You may wonder why the Apostle Paul places the emphasis upon the name Christ rather than the name Jesus. It is significant that the name Christ is used here, so that no one deny that Jesus and Christ are the same—that is to say, God manifest in the flesh. It was Christ who took a body, it was Christ who died in that body, it was Christ who rose in that body, it was Christ who ascended in that body, it is Christ who is present at the right hand of God the Father interceding for us, and it is Christ who is coming again—the Man Christ Jesus. Do not try to separate Jesus and Christ and make two persons because they are not two persons, they are One.

If the dead do not rise from the grave, then Christ did not rise from the dead. We cannot imagine the results, the consequences, had not Christ risen from the dead. In the 17th verse of 1 Corinthians, chapter 15, Paul says that if Christ did not rise from the dead, your faith is nothing and you are still in your sins. That peace that you imagine you have because of your faith in the Lord Jesus Christ is the result of self-deceit, your sins are not forgiven, you have no peace, you have no joy, you have no true happiness, you have no hope, you have no eternal prospects unless Christ rose from the dead. You are still in your sins, you are lost, doomed, you are on your way out into oblivion—a land from where there is no return, from where there has come no word, an experience of which nobody knows anything—unless Christ was risen from the dead. Those who have died as his children are perished. The dead in Christ shall not rise if the dead do not rise; and all of your loved ones, all of the Old Testament saints, all of the New Testament saints who died in faith are perished, gone forever, doomed, never again to be seen or known by anyone else—unless Christ rose from the dead. If in this life only we have hope in Christ; if Christ just means a little peace and a little joy, a little forgiveness and a quiet conscience in this life, if that is all there is to Christianity, then, the Apostle Paul says, we are of all men most miserable.

But the Apostle Paul does not allow his message to come to a close on that note. 1 Corinthians 15:20 says, "But in fact Christ has been raised from the dead." It is an established, historical, documented fact that Christ rose visibly, bodily, literally, tangibly from the dead and ascended into heaven in that same way; and from there we look for him in that visible, bodily, literal, tangible return when he comes to claim his own in that special resurrection—the resurrection out from among the dead.

The Apostle Paul gives his reader much to think about concerning what to expect after this earthly life when he penned the fifteenth chapter of 1 Corinthians. In writing to the church in Corinth in verses 51 and 52 he writes these words: "Behold! I tell you a mystery. We shall not all sleep, but we shall all be changed, in a moment, in the twinkling of an eye, at the last trumpet. For the trumpet will sound, and the dead will be raised imperishable, and we shall be changed." In the oldest preserved manuscripts there are considerable differences expressed by theologians on these verses—some contradicting the text we have today by eliminating the first *not*. They make it read, "We shall all sleep, but not all shall be changed." These changes arose out of dislike of what was implied because it made it difficult for them to reconcile what is said here with what is said in the Book of Hebrews, "it is appointed for man to die once." "How then" they ask, "if all men are to die, can it be true that some are not to die?" The difficulty is solved by seeing that the author (whom I believe to be the Apostle Paul), is there in Hebrews speaking of what is appointed to fallen man, unredeemed, and under judgment. We say this because he goes on to say, "After death comes judgment." He is not speaking there of what he is saying here in 1 Corinthians 15—a mystery or secret not before revealed—except of what was revealed to Adam and his sons ever since the Fall.

What is meant by "mystery?" In the English we usually mean something not cleared up or something unintelligible. But that is not the sense of the word in Scripture. In the New Testament mystery signifies what was once a secret of God alone, but is now revealed. It does not mean "what cannot be understood"; on the contrary, the revelation given concerning it makes it perfectly capable of being understood. Next the apostle proceeds to deal with the kind of body in which we will be raised.

However holy a man may be, even if he were the Apostle Paul himself, his body is but flesh and blood, which is unsuited for the heavenly places and for an eternity of life. And if the bodies of the living believers are unfit for it, how much more the bodies of the departed, whose remains are decaying in the ground. The believers at Corinth were confused. The Apostle Paul answers that some believers will be found alive on earth when Christ comes. "We shall not all sleep." That is also what the apostle was saying in 1 Thessalonians 4, where the believers of that region thought that only the living would be able to have part in the millennial kingdom. In that chapter he had spoken of the rapture of both the living and the dead. But he had not spoken of their bodies. The Thessalonian believers were confused concerning the dead believers. In 1 Corinthians 15, Paul calls them "the sleepers in Christ," whom Christ will easily awaken. This physical hindrance will be shaken off in a moment by the miraculous action of Christ. And while some will be found still alive at the moment of Christ's coming, a change must take place upon their bodies, as well as on the bodies of the dead, in order to prepare them for the glory of eternity. "We must all be changed."

The "all" does not mean "all mankind." The apostle is speaking of believers. Scripture distinguishes resurrection, but up until one hundred fifty years ago it was believed that prophecy did not typically make a distinction between the first and the second resurrections. The Reformers were content to mainly focus upon the primary question concerning the salvation of sinners. Resurrection was one great act occurring at the same moment for the saved and the lost. Everyone was to rise, and there, in the presence of Christ, were for the first time, perceptibly, and eternally to be distinguished. When Paul says, "We shall all be changed in a moment" he is referring to believers. It is they alone who will be change. "In the twinkling of an eye," describes the instant as it affects those still alive in the flesh on earth. These arise into the air to have their soul and new body knit together. When the dead in Christ come out of their graves it will be at the signal of the trumpet of God. Their bodies will be eternal and will never again see decay. The change, then, is at once to fit the believer for his entry into the Presence of Christ.

Do not allow yourself to be deceived into believing that there is no bodily resurrection, that only the soul is resurrected at death. That is not the teaching of the Bible. Those who are spiritists, who do not allow for the resurrection of the body, do so on grounds counter to what God says on numerous occasions in Scripture. Resurrection in Scripture is the undoing of death, the coming forth of the body out of the tomb in which it was laid. Jesus says as much in the Gospel of John 5:28, 29, "Do not marvel at this, for an hour is coming when all who are in the tombs will hear his voice and come out, those who have done good to the resurrection of life, and those who have done evil to the resurrection of judgment." All rise; at different times, but all rise. Four times we have in Scripture "put on," in relation to the resurrection.

Concerning the time of resurrection, Scripture speaks of resurrection as about to take place at a future day, and at an unknown time. It is to be a breaking in upon the ordinary course of things on earth at an instant—not by the powers of nature, but by the power of God. To this end, Christ is to descend, and by his mighty call and miraculous power he will summon his own. Those who refuse the Bible's proof of bodily resurrection tend to believe that there is no wrath at all in God. They believe he never will inflict the torments of Hell on his enemies. In their view, there is no future judgment for the dead who are now assembled in Sheol. They say each one, as soon as he dies, continues to experience the enjoyments he found while alive. Each is to do his best, and that will suffice for God. Therefore, the doctrine of the thousand years, and of the reward to God's faithful servants, can have no place with them. God's threatening of wrath against transgressors is not to be believed. All at death, whether good or evil, depart this life in spirit-form, never to be reunited with the body.

In Scripture, on the other hand, we see that the Son of God is to assemble to himself the righteous a thousand years before he raises the wicked dead out of their graves. If there is not to be a bodily resurrection, the Apostle Paul's doctrine given in response to troubles which surfaced at Thessalonica, would have been written very differently in reply. They were troubled, because, as they thought, believers who were already dead would have no part in the kingdom of Christ at his appearing.

The Apostle Paul's views were far from those of spiritists. He assures the Thessalonians that death was no obstacle to the entrance into this future glory. As death had been endured and shaken off by Christ, so its chains will in a moment be broken by the Lord's people. Both the living and the dead of Christ's saints will together be caught up in clouds to meet Christ who is descending. The apostle assures us, that by reason of the state of their bodies, both living and dead believers are unfit for the coming kingdom of God's glory.

The worst part of death for the unbeliever is not the natural pains of departure; not the disruption of earthly ties. It is the sense that death is God's divine displeasure. Passing into the dark beyond is accompanied with dread. But more awful still is the thought of having to go into the presence of a God to whom man has so often offended. It is sad in the case of an infant, to see death where there is only the attachment of original sin. But that trouble is increased, when to the Fall men have added frequent transgressions against God. The consequence of our transgressions is the deepest where the gospel has been heard and ignored. That person is dying without hope, and can expect to meet the God of justice, unforgiven. "The sting of death is sin;" and one of the chief of sins, is the putting-off or despising the gospel of God's grace.

CHAPTER 7

Putting On Your Immortal Body

In 1 Corinthians 15:53 we find a couple of key expressions that Paul used to describe what happens to our body when we are raptured into the air to be with Christ. Paul says in 1 Thessalonians 4:16 and 17, "For the Lord himself will descend from heaven with a cry of command, with the voice of an archangel, and with the sound of the trumpet of God. And the dead in Christ will rise first. Then we who are alive, who are left, will be caught up together with them in the clouds to meet the Lord in the air, and so we will always be with the Lord." Recall that when we die, our bodies—which are suited for life in this world and are perishable and mortal—are buried in the ground with the decaying things of earth. Our soul and spirit, however, live on and are immediately brought into Sheol. It is the place of temporary holding for all human beings upon death. But the saved and the unsaved are separated by a physical barrier or void preventing them from having contact with each other. In Sheol there is physical torment for the person who has died without accepting Christ's gift of salvation. The unbeliever will long for relief from his torment, but never experience it. The opposite is true of the believer in Christ's forgiveness and redemption. For this person, there is a heightened consciousness of Christ and longing to be in his presence in heaven.

At an unknown moment in time, Christ will descend from heaven—as the Apostle Paul describes for us in 1 Thessalonians 4—and call-out to all the living and the dead who are his by faith. The spirit and soul of those believers who have died and are residing in Sheol will ascend to meet him. The body, spirit and soul of each living believer will likewise ascend into the air to meet Christ. For those who are residing in Sheol and are unbelievers, they will remain there for release at a future time. Notice that the believers who are still alive at the time of Christ's appearing are ascending with body, spirit and soul intact, while those arriving from Sheol will be reunited with their bodies so that they are once again made complete in body, spirit and soul. God's intent is that we should enter heaven in the same three-part completeness with which we were originally made.

It is at that moment of rapture into the air that 1 Corinthians 15, verse 53 takes place—"For this perishable body must put on the imperishable, and this mortal body must put on immortality." It represents the moment of resurrection; the time of the rapture and its reconnecting of the body to the soul and spirit. It is here that we need to be careful not to think of the acquisition of this new body as a casting off of the old and replacement with the new. There is a kind of amalgamation that takes place; a stirring together of both the old and new so that there remains recognizable aspects of who you are, just as Christ was recognizable at his resurrection, yet had new bodily characteristics. The old body by itself is not fit for heaven and its requirements, and so a new covering has to be given. We are carefully informed by the Apostle Paul that there is no replacement of old body for new because the perishable must "put on" and not be replaced by a new body. Additionally, he says that "this" perishable body must put on the imperishable. In describing the transition in this way he gives further indication of our present physical form and its limitation for use in heaven.

In verse 54, the Apostle Paul says that, "When the perishable puts on the imperishable, and the mortal puts on immortality, then shall come to pass the saying that is written: 'Death is swallowed up in victory.'" Notice when the victory is won. There are those who want to elevate death into the place assigned by Scripture for the moment of resurrection. They expect to die and immediately have the victory of resurrection and then entrance into heaven. They say that death is the point of demarcation from earth to heaven. But the Scriptures speak of no such thing. The Scriptures speak of resurrection, not death, as the Christian's triumph. Death, even in the believer's case, gives the perception that it steals life. It is true that death has been conquered by Christ for the believer, and as the Apostle Paul writes, its sting is taken away. 1 Corinthians 15:55 says, "O death, where is your victory? O death, where is your sting?" Nevertheless, the moment of death does not represent, in itself, the ultimate victory because a believer's death does not create an immediate ascent to the glory of God into heaven; it cannot since God uses death as merely an *unclothing* in order to *reclothe* with the appropriate body for use in heaven. It is an *unclothing* because the soul and spirit are separated from the body by death. God will not visibly own his sons and daughters until they are completely free from the effects of the curse of sin. The body of the believer is as much the slave of corruption, as the body of the godless. As God created us to be body, spirit and soul, his desire is to welcome the believer into heaven in the same complete manner.

The Apostle Paul describes death for the believer as "falling asleep." But sleep is not the victory, though it is a necessary step forward to victory. Death is not victory because a man's soul immediately goes into the custody of Sheol (or Hades in the Greek). He is identified as a prisoner—although a prisoner of hope. And though, as the Apostle Paul says, to depart is to be with Christ, which is far better than life, he is also aware that his body is detained in the chains of the last enemy we call death. Death is at present a feeling of sorrow. In a real sense death is an occasion of sorrow for the Church because it has lost a soldier in the fight against sin. He is struck down and carried to the grave, no longer able to take part in the conflict.

The true moment of victory is resurrection. Death is an unclothing; part of the penalty of sin. But resurrection is a victory, and it is the vehicle for *re-clothing*. It is the untethering by Divine power of those who have become prisoners of death—of the body released from the tomb, and the soul and spirit released from Sheol. And while to some death of the body is perceived to be an immediate and complete victory, to Scripture the only real victory is what it calls the "putting on" of a body that is made incorruptible.

Notice that imperishable, and immortality, refer not to

the soul, but to the body—or rather to man as a whole. Scripture does not speak of the natural immortality of the soul, but of the imperishable of the dead at resurrection. Scripture promises that the body and soul of the person will be rejoined, never again to be parted. The expression is: "Then shall take place." The Greek word here means—"at that time." The expression refers to a future moment, which immediately affects both the living and the dead believer. In order that death's hold may be utterly ripped away, it is not enough that the dead alone should rise and be clothed with bodies inaccessible to corruption, because living believers also carry bodies which contain the seeds of death. Therefore, at the moment of resurrection for the dead in Sheol, the living must also simultaneously experience the putting on of a body that is made incorruptible. In a broad sense, salvation is not truly made complete until death, which is the effect of the curse; because with death sin for the believer is blotted completely out, the scars of sin removed, and the bondage to sin overcome.

When the Apostle Paul declares that "death is swallowed up in victory," he has taken it from Isaiah 25. That particular chapter is a declaration of the events of the end-times on the earth. It is a period of divine activity which includes horrifying suffering. Nevertheless, the believer will have been resurrected beforehand. To adequately understand this and other prophecies in the Book of Isaiah, the doctrine of the millennium (the thousand years with Christ upon earth) must be understood and taken into account. Without the millennium as a key, the prophets are unintelligible since their prophecies must be viewed as a connected whole which includes "the great and terrible Day of the Lord," (Joel 2:31) and the coming of Christ and His kingdom during that day.

Isaiah 24 describes God's judgment of the whole earth, without respect of people. It gives the state of the world when struck by the end-time judgments of God's wrath. The declaration God made to Noah—the promise that God would never again flood the earth—will be ended. This divine prediction is what gave the earth the regularity of the seasons. But when God sets out in the future to bring destruction upon the earth, the world will be a place without seasons; instead it will be one of sorrow. Joy will have left it. Only a small remnant out of the billions of earth's inhabitants will survive. That day will be a fearful one for the nonbeliever which ends in the earth's utter annihilation. Yet, for the believer it is a non-experience because he is safely in heaven.

The Apostle Paul asks, "O death, where is your victory? O death, where is your sting?" This is likely a quotation from the Old Testament prophet Hosea. Words to this effect are found in the Book of Hosea 13:14. The context describes the time when God, because of idolatry, was rejecting the tribes of Israel. Yet, amid the announcement of judgment, there are promises of final mercy in Hosea 2:18–23. The Lord, when led to death, describes the time of terrible trouble which will overtake Israel and the world because of their disobedience. Hosea 10:8 says, "The high places of Aven, the sin of Israel, shall be destroyed. Thorn and thistle shall grow up on their altars, and they shall say to the mountains, Cover us, and to the hills, Fall on us." In this prophetic book we also find God's love through Christ as the representative of Israel (Hosea 11:1).

At the close of this present age, Christ himself steps onto the scene of Israel's self-made ruin, and will be their King (Hosea 13:9). Then comes a ransom from Sheol and the tomb—as described in Hosea 13:14. The Apostle Paul borrows from these words when he says that death and its sting will be taken away by the work of Christ. These words, then, are the joyous cry of the believers held captive when they are released out of Sheol where they have been long held. They will have forever passed beyond death and its power. Risen from the dead, they are beyond temptations and the sin which now inflicts those who are alive. They escape out of Sheol—a place which kept them so long from their hopes of heaven. Recall Revelation 6:9, 10: "When he opened the fifth seal, I saw under the altar the souls of those who had been slain for the word of God and for the witness they had borne. They cried out with a loud voice, 'O Sovereign Lord, holy and true, how long before you will judge and avenge our blood on those who dwell on the earth?'"

Through the actions of Christ, "the gates of Sheol" shall then no longer prevail against his people (as it reads in Matthew 16.18). It is then that the "putting on" of the imperishable will take place. It is the clothing over our old body with the body of immortality that is the longing of those who are held captive in Sheol. Entrance into heaven and into the full presence of Christ cannot take place without this resurrection event. The very end of the Bible says—"He who testifies to these things says, 'Surely I am coming soon.' Amen. Come, Lord Jesus!" Let that be our longing.

CHAPTER 8

Your Heavenly Homes

We have traced the biblical sequence of events that lead from the moment of death to the resurrection of our new body and its uniting with our spirit and soul. With this final reunion we are made ready to enter into heaven. When the spirit, soul, and body are granted entry into heaven to be with Christ, we will be in a perfect, sinless form for eternal enjoyment. But, entry into heaven and into the full presence of Christ where he now resides is not our final destination. Entry into heaven gives us full presence with Christ and worship of Christ that is longed-for, but it is not the final location of our place of residence. Earth is that final location—a new, glorified, sinless, eternal earth. We will once again return to earth; this time with a sinless character, and this time with none of the present cares of earth to distract us from the true intended focus of our affection. At the end of this age, when the last judgment (referred to in Scripture as "the White Throne of Judgment") takes place our new and final home will be made ready. But first, several things must take place, and like the previous enlightenments in this book, it is all discoverable in the Scriptures.

In this life Christians strive for heaven—or, at least it is intended that they should be striving. Perhaps one of the chief reasons so many Christians do not strive for heaven is that they hear so little theological discussion about its importance. Christians hear so few sermons on heaven and the afterlife. The Bible speaks repeatedly of this world as a place of sojourn and pilgrimage. Yet Sunday after Sunday many churches preach the reward of prosperity and well-being in its various forms in the hear and now. Christians are taught to focus upon grasping hold of God and pulling expectantly on him for help in this life's trials and circumstances. That, however, was not always the focus of the church. Christians were once taught to long for God—not in this life—but in the eternal life to come. They were taught to live with a longing to see God face-to-face. The Catholic Church termed it "Beatific Vision." Protestant denominations referred to it as "Christian Perfection." The Apostle Paul said in 1 Corinthians 13:12, "For now we see in a mirror dimly, but then face to face. Now I know in part; then I shall know fully, even as I have been fully known." In this mortal, fleeting life the aim of the fully surrendered Christian ought to be to long to see God face-to-face in heaven. Still, in this life, we can only long to see God. The Apostle Paul reminds Timothy in 1 Timothy 6:16 that God dwells in unapproachable light, "whom no one has ever seen or can see." That is true in this life, but not when we receive our resurrected body and are ushered into heaven; because then, we *will* see God face-to-face in heaven.

The word heaven occurs hundreds of times in the Old Testament and the New. It's meaning, whether translated from the Hebrew or the Greek, nearly always literally means "that which is above." And even though we are reminded in the Scriptures that the "heaven of heavens cannot contain God," and that God is present everywhere, on earth as well as in heaven, nevertheless, the same Scriptures clearly teach that God does particularly dwell in heaven. As you read through the Scriptures you will discover that heaven is referred to with seven different words which give as their meaning a dwelling or habitation. The words are: tabernacle, dwelling place, sanctuary, habitation, house, temple, and the throne of God. All of these synonyms have one basic characteristic: *holiness*. The Book of Habakkuk says, "the LORD is in his holy temple; let all the earth keep silence before him." (2:20). To speak of heaven as a dwelling place connotes individuals in intimate relationship with one another. This vast group of people in heaven will enjoy the most precious fellowship with God and one another—in contrast to the shallow enjoyments experienced here on earth. Our fellowship will last forever, never to be interrupted by sickness or death. But that enjoyment will not always be in heaven as our home.

When the Psalms refer to sanctuary, the temple, or the house of God, the psalmist typically has in mind something more than a literal dwelling place—as the Israelite might have perceived the expression to mean. For example, the Israelite might have thought the expression in Psalm 23, "I shall dwell in the house of the Lord forever," to mean a literal dwelling. But, when Psalm 84:2 says, "My soul longs, yes, faints for the courts of the LORD; my heart and flesh sing for joy to the living God," it expresses the thought of venturing into the presence of God in true fellowship.

Therefore, our concern must not be for the *location* where God is to be found, so much as *that* he is found and to worship in his presence for all eternity. More importantly, heaven would not be longed for were it not for the fact that that is where Christ is to be found.

We have insisted in this book that no believers occupy heaven at the present time. Yet, there are inhabitants there already: the angels. Of all the supernatural beings that the Scriptures mention, it is the angels who are regularly identified with heaven. They are referred to as the heavenly hosts. For example, when Jacob had his vision at Bethel, he saw a ladder reaching up to heaven and angels in large numbers descending and ascending on it. Jesus himself spoke of "the angels in heaven." Because angels are spirits they normally are identified without bodies, but at times they assume bodies for purposes ordained by God, and as such are sometimes confused for men. They are an innumerable number. Still, they will be outnumbered by believers when they ascend into heaven with their resurrected bodies. Unlike the angels, believers will not be in heaven as spirits. They will be there in bodily form.

Before we look into the question of whether heaven is a believer's final home, we should ask another puzzling question. What will believers do in heaven? The Scriptures do not give us much information about what the redeemed of Christ will be doing in heaven. Therefore, what is mentioned must be considered to be very important to our understanding. One of the most obvious and continuous activities will be the worship of God in his full godhood: Father, Son, and Holy Spirit. Perhaps the best place in Scripture to discover this activity is in the opening part of chapter 19 of the Book of Revelation:

> After this I heard what seemed to be the loud voice of a great multitude in heaven, crying out, "Hallelujah! Salvation and glory and power belong to our God, for his judgments are true and just; for he has judged the great prostitute who corrupted the earth with her immorality, and has avenged on her the blood of his servants." Once more they cried out, "Hallelujah! The smoke from her goes up forever and ever." And the twenty-four elders and the four living creatures fell down and worshiped God who was seated on the throne, saying, "Amen. Hallelujah!" And from the throne came a voice saying, "Praise our God, all you his servants, you who fear him, small and great." Then I heard what seemed to be the voice of a great multitude, like the roar of many waters and like the sound of mighty peals of thunder, crying out, "Hallelujah! For the Lord our God the Almighty reigns. Let us rejoice and exult and give him the glory, for the marriage of the Lamb has come, and his Bride has made herself ready; it was granted her to clothe herself with fine linen, bright and pure"—for the fine linen is the righteous deeds of the saints.

The worship of God mentioned elsewhere in Scripture will surely have its fulfillment in heaven. Psalm 29:2, for example, says that we should ascribe to the Lord the glory due his name and worship him in the splendor of holiness. It appears that much of this worship, if not all, will be offered with music. The Book of Revelation—which contains more songs than any book of the Bible—is the book that speaks of end time events and future glory in heaven. Fourteen of the psalms are also sung by groups in heaven.

The last chapter of the Bible includes this sentence: "and his servants will serve him." The verb "to serve" means to serve in a worshipful manner. In the Book of Revelation it is not the common verb form of the word *serve* but a less common form used to refer to those who serve in the Temple or in the House of God. A prominent theologian once recounted for me the time he was explaining to an audience the service to be performed for God in heaven. A women responded, "I'm old and tired. I don't want to work." Her earthly mindset was obviously misguided. She didn't take into account that the body she is to receive will be fit for heaven. Work in heaven is free from care, toil and fatigue. It is furthermore, work according to one's tastes and ability—the activities that provide contentment that God has uniquely designed within you. We will rest, but it will be rest from sin, rest from suffering. We will rest with God with a perfect soul and body enjoying God in perfect rest as God himself will rest in his love for us. The Book of Zephaniah says of God, "The Lord your God is in your midst, a mighty one who will save; he will rejoice over you with gladness; he will quiet you by his love; he will exult over you with loud singing."

There is also fellowship in heaven. In this world our friendships are limited by time and distance. There are those in this world with whom we might have had friendship if we lived in their moment in time, people who you believe would have been like-minded and shared identical views of God and life; people with whom you might have shared the closest friendships had you had the opportunity to meet them. In heaven there is no separation by distance—either in time or location. The ultimate enjoyment of these friendships in heaven will be to collectively direct our common thoughts to the great works of God. We will pass through eternity in deepening appreciation of the works of God. Learning of God will consume us.

To deepen our appreciation and love of God we must know more about God. So heaven will also be a place of learning. In this earth-life we know little about God. What we know comes mainly from the Scriptures, from nature and what he reveals about himself through meditation and answered prayer. As Christ taught us to know and love the Father in this life, how much more will he teach us about his Father in the heaven-life. But where will all this learning take place? Where will the fellowship and worship take place? In heaven? Only for a time, because heaven will pass away.

As time concludes—or as theology states it, the "consummation" occurs—there will be a new heaven and a new earth. The first time we are introduced in Scripture to the occurrence of a new heaven and earth is at the end of the Book of Isaiah. The prophet is allowed to see not only the earthly opposition to the coming kingdom of God, but he also witnesses the transformation of earth and the heavens above. The statement contained in the book is brief: "For behold, I create new heavens and a new earth, and the former things shall not be remembered or come into mind." (Isaiah 65:17). Similar words are spoken in Isaiah 66:22: "For as the new heavens and the new earth that I make shall remain before me, says the LORD, so shall your offspring and your name remain." The second clause of Isaiah 65:17 literally reads: "and it shall not come up upon the heart." It's a fascinating expression. It simply means that the splendor of the new heaven and earth will be so satisfying that there will be no wishing for the remembrances of the old. This may be what the psalmist had in mind in Psalm 102:26 when he said, "They will perish, but you will remain; they will all wear out like a garment. You will change them like a robe, and they will pass away." The author of the Book of Hebrews uses similar language in Hebrews 1:11, 12 when he says, "they will perish, but you remain; they will all wear out like a garment, like a robe you will roll them up, like a garment they will be changed. But you are the same, and your years will have no end."

The final reference to a new heaven and earth in Scripture occurs at the end of the Book of Revelation, in 21:1, where it reads, "Then I saw a new heaven and a new earth, for the first heaven and the first earth had passed away, and the sea was no more." This takes place at the conclusion of the millennial reign and the final disposition of Satan and the judgment of the Great White Throne. When verse 1 uses the word *new* it is the Greek word that means not new in time, but new in quality. The old is replaced with something better—just like our resurrected body. It is likely that 2 Peter 3:7 is also speaking of the new heaven and earth: "But by the same word the heavens and earth that now exist are stored up for fire, being kept until the day of judgment and destruction of the ungodly." All that exists upon and within the earth will be consumed without the loss of any existing matter. All will be melted, refined and purified from the contamination of sin. The earth, surrounded by a new heaven (or atmosphere), will be adapted to the nature and requirements of sinless beings. Earth will become the residence of the righteous. And here the Scriptures become silent as to the mode of existence there. But we may be certain that like the present world the new one will be a material existence. There will be a solid sphere and a transparent expanse (heaven) around it. The proper heaven itself—the place of residence of God—is not made new because it has never been corrupted by sin. It remains the same. Yet out of heaven will flow a new city, a holy city suspended over the earth, made perfect for the righteous inhabitants of earth. It's size and location will be perfectly established to contain all who will reside there. These are the words of Horatius Bonar (*Light and Truth*, 1872):

> Blessed city! City of peace, and love, and song! Fit accompaniment of the new heavens! Fit metropolis of the new earth, wherein dwelleth righteousness! How eagerly should we look for it! How worthy of it should we live! It has not yet arrived. Eye hath not seen it. But God points to it above, and assures us that it shall come.

Believers have the right of citizenship to this new earth and residence now; and they who are to dwell in it are not angels, but fallen men. Yet, access to this new home comes with an application. Christ said "I go to prepare a place for you." (John 14:2). Christ is its Builder and Maker, and he gives it freely. Nevertheless, it was bought with a price. He who is its Maker, whose blood has bought and opened it, gives it freely. He waits to receive our application. What's more, he earnestly invites us to apply. He announces that whomever will take him at his word, and trust him for entrance into it, will receive it. It is Christ's shed blood on the cross that brings us into our eternal relationship and grants entry through the gates of the city. It will be a joy to enter that jubilant city. It is imperative that you secure your citizenship here and now!

APPENDIX

The Life-changing Gospel

Often there is an event in life that becomes defining; a microcosm of one's character and life on full display. The Bible does the same thing. Anyone who reads through the pages of the Bible also finds their life on full display. The Bible does many things, and one of the most important things it does is convict. That is why in this day and age we find so few people coming through the doorway of a church that opens the Bible and preaches from it. But that is a dangerous thing to avoid. We are entering into darker times in the world, and at an increasingly greater pace. As people move away from God and closer to their own self-interests they are increasingly less likely to want to open the Bible and stare into the face of God. Knowledge of God comes from his Bible. Without biblical knowledge there is no appeal to salvation; and without salvation there is no hope for eternity with God. The Bible says in the Gospel of John, "This is the judgment: the light has come into the world, and people loved the darkness rather than the light because their deeds were evil." And it also says, in 2 Peter 3:3, "that scoffers will come in the last days with scoffing, following their own sinful desires."

The gospel message, once accepted, becomes the great turning point of each life because it is designed to answer all human needs. It is intended to display our character to ourselves, to others, and to God. Whether we believe it or disbelieve it, accept or neglect it, it shows the state of our heart as good or evil more clearly and more deeply than anything else. Additionally, the Bible is intended to affect a change in our character from evil to good, and to work a change in it so vast that our character will be made new. The most terrible fears, the brightest hopes, are all made known to us in the Bible. The strongest condemnation of sin is there, and yet the most appealing display of love on the part of God is there—founded on God's atonement for sinners, in his Son.

The Bible is intended also to produce a permanent change in our condition. It is the most glorious offer that can be made to sinful man. The acceptance of it yields eternal life; the rejection of it everlasting death. The gospel is intended to be the great turning point in everyone's life. Unless it reveals a person's character as a sinner he will never seek nor feel the need of a Savior. It must change a person's character or else he will always be an unbelieving soul lost for eternity. And lastly, it must change a person's future life, because that life by nature leads to death. It must bring him from under the condemnation and curse of the law, to the blessings and enjoyments of reconciliation and pardon with God.

Yet, there comes with this truth an important corresponding responsibility. We know what is meant by responsibility in everyday life. We know that responsibility is intended to make us more earnest in applying ourselves. Similarly, the gospel provides us information about the circumstances of our life, and it marks out our proper course. The gospel either increases our guilt, or it brings freedom and deliverance from it.

The Apostle Paul says in Hebrews 2:3, "How shall we escape if we neglect such a great salvation?" The gospel introduces us to the guilt of a sinful life. It is set before us with Paul's straight-forward question. We might equate the death of a sinner as the consequence of his sin. He stands trial before God and we ask, "How can he escape?" In his sin he would justly deserve to die. No reason could be offered before God as judge as to why he should be spared. No excuse can be made before God. How will you answer God when God approaches in mercy; when he reasons with you, and by his Son he calls out to you to be reconciled and saved; when he places in your hands and before your eyes the hope of pardon and promise. And with all this many will leave this life regarding every bit of his love as nothing. How will you answer him? "How will you escape if you neglect such a great salvation?"

We are clearly told that from our birth we are exposed to the inevitable wrath of God. From birth we are already condemned. Our life is entirely in the hands of God. But, into this state of despair comes the message of mercy. To reject God's mercy is eternal madness. The most common form of sin against the life-saving news of eternal life, is neglect. Neglect proves that the heart is by nature evil and cold toward God. The Lord left his throne to become our Redeemer. He appeared in the likeness of man to bear our sin in anguish on the cross. He offered us pardon for our sin. Yet, this wealth of love, this overflowing of mercy, is treated with coldness and indifference. Pardon is freely given, despite our former sins, if we only believe his message.

Many people look at themselves and see goodness. They say, "I've always tried to do good." If it were true, it still could not help them. They convince themselves that they have the hope of salvation but neglect Christ's gospel. This verse convicts them: "How shall you escape if you neglect such a great salvation?" Neglect is enough. They say that they personify "goodness." God calls it neglect. They think they are not in danger. The Apostle Paul thought they were and that they had no excuse and no escape. God the Creator, God the Redeemer, God the Judge, asks solemnly and in mercy: "How will you escape, if you neglect such a great salvation?" Even an apostle such as Paul fails to tell the greatness of the gospel news. As God when he swears, swears "by himself, because he can swear by no greater," so Paul speaking by the Spirit of the deliverance of the gospel, can find nothing with which to compare it; and so he sets it by itself—"So great a salvation"

There is such a great salvation that lays hold of the children of Adam to pluck them from the grave and the eternal fire of hell. Through Christ Jesus, man—ignorant, sleeping, defiled, dying—is aroused from his sleep and carried from this life into the inheritance of the mansions of God. Great is the salvation of Christ. Angels fly here and there, carrying the joyful message, but demons are in stealthy flight aiming to hinder the message and lay ambush. Why was the world beneath our feet and the sky over our heads fixed? Here's why: As a platform for the great scene of salvation; as a battlefield upon which Satan and his hosts will be routed, and man will be released from his sinful bondage.

And it is deeper and still more profound than that. Great is such a salvation, because great is the damnation from which it rescues. Israel's deliverance was great because the labor of Egypt's brick-kilns was heavy, and the toil and the task exhausting and cruel. Vast then, beyond measure, is the salvation of Christ. As Satan the fallen angel is greater in might, and cruelty, and cunning than Pharaoh, so is his service absolute slavery, and his wages death. Great is its salvation, because the price paid is great. Who can comprehend worth when that worth is infinite? Count the sands of the seashores, if it were possible. Go count the number of the stars. Yet, were every grain of sand the value of gold the price of our ransom would still pale in significance.

The Bible says the church of God was obtained with his own blood. Think of that great salvation. Great is our salvation in its deep mystery. "God manifested in the flesh"— for our sake the Ruler of creation a slave for our salvation, the Lord of life bowing to death. Great is our salvation.

To the lost, Christ a Savior; to the sick, Christ a physician; to the ignorant, Christ a prophet; to the frail, Christ a champion; to the forgotten, Christ a friend; to the blind, Christ the giver of sight; to the hungry, Christ the bread of life. Neglect this great salvation and the very greatness of salvation will press with a mountain force on your chest; will be the unanswerable reason for your eternal death. Slight so great a salvation, and you must perish. Nothing can save you. The judgment day will yield only your doom. Then you will choke out sobs of unutterable sorrow.

How could you then sue for mercy, when a lifetime has been spent in despising it? To whom will you turn, as an advocate? The Lamb that died for you has turned to wrath. And if the very Lamb displays his wrath to you, who will dare act on your behalf? Your knowledge of Christ's gospel will cover you with shame. Your neglect of his love will quiet your speechless tongue. Self-condemned, your lips will quiver with fear. Ingratitude will spread despair over your face. The Bible says in the Book of Isaiah, "The sinners in Zion are afraid; trembling has seized the godless: 'Who among us can dwell with the consuming fire? Who among us can dwell with everlasting burnings?'"